jazz country

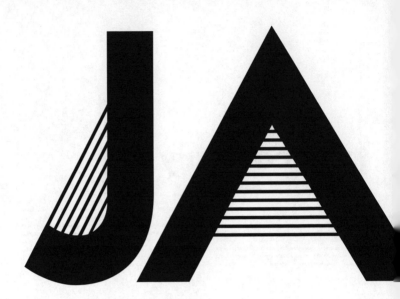

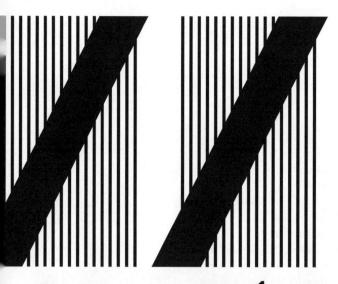

country

Ralph Ellison in America

HORACE A. PORTER

UNIVERSITY OF IOWA PRESS 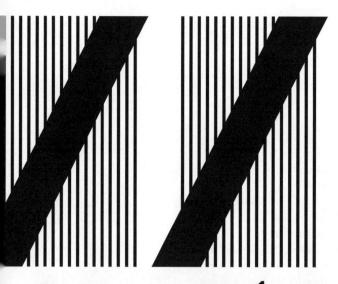 IOWA CITY

University of Iowa Press, Iowa City 52242
Printed in the United States of America
Design by Richard Hendel
http://www.uiowa.edu/~uipress

A version of chapter 1 was previously published
as "Jazz Beginnings: Ralph Ellison and Charlie
Christian in Oklahoma City" in the *Antioch Review* 57
(Summer 1999).

The publication of this book was generously
supported by the University of Iowa Foundation.

Printed on acid-free paper

Library of Congress Cataloging-in-Publication Data
Porter, Horace A., 1950–
    Jazz country: Ralph Ellison in America / by
    Horace A. Porter.
        p.   cm.
    Includes bibliographical references and index.
    ISBN 0-87745-777-8 (cloth)
    1. Jazz in literature. 2. Ellison, Ralph —
    Knowledge — Jazz. I. Title.
ML80.E45 P67   2001
818'.5409 — DC21   2001027538

01 02 03 04 05 C 5 4 3 2 1

For Zachary E. Porter

It makes no difference if it's sweet or hot,
Just keep that rhythm,
Give it everything you've got!

It don't mean a thing
If it ain't got that swing!

—Duke Ellington

Contents

Acknowledgments

Jazz Country was at first a longer book which grew more succinct and meditative along the way. I owe thanks to several excellent readers who forced me to meditate somewhat longer than I had planned. Professor Louis Renza, my friend and former colleague at Dartmouth, read the first version of the manuscript and made powerful suggestions. Jeannette Hopkins, a wonderful editor and friend, also read two early drafts and forced me to make more sense. Arnold Rampersad helped me yet again by microscopically reading the manuscript near its completion. I offer praise and special thanks to Holly Carver, Prasenjit Gupta, Charlotte Wright, and Megan Scott of the University of Iowa Press. They were superb. Thanks to Gail Zlatnik for magically copy-editing the book. Peter Brigaitis and Marie S. Nuchols created a fine index.

The book represents my own rendition of a long trumpet solo. While writing I felt as though I were sitting in the company of Albert Murray, Robert G. O'Meally, James Alan McPherson, John F. Callahan, Jerry Watts, Arnold Rampersad, and Lawrence Jackson. Their writings and comments about Ellison have been extremely valuable to me.

One summer afternoon in Vermont, Jay and Lois Wright offered me a crash course on jazz. Thanks also, Jay, for your transformative commentary on the manuscript. Special thanks to Jerry Watts—from New Haven to now. Larry Jackson, "props" to you. A salute to George Harding for his encouragement.

Carla Carr, my spouse, read various drafts of the manuscript and offered her love and help throughout. Finally, my son Zack, who shares Ellison's birthday and to whom this book is dedicated, kept me honest and entertained with his witty comments. Cheers to all.

Chronology

March 1, 1914
Ellison is born in Oklahoma City, Oklahoma.

1917
Ellison's father, Lewis Alfred Ellison, dies.

1922
Ellison studies the trumpet.

1933
Enrolls in Tuskegee Institute in Tuskegee, Alabama; plans to major in music.

1936
Takes up the study of sculpture in New York City.

1937
Ellison's mother, Ida Milsap, dies; he is introduced to Richard Wright by Langston Hughes; first review published in *New Challenge*.

1938
Becomes a writer with the Federal Writers' Project.

1939–1941
Publishes several short stories.

1942
Becomes editor of *Negro Quarterly*.

1943–1945
Serves in the Merchant Marines.

1945
Recipient of grant from the Rosenwald Foundation; starts work on draft of *Invisible Man*.

1946
Marries Fanny McConnell.

1952
Invisible Man published by Random House.

1953
Ellison receives National Book Award and National Newspaper Publishers' Russwurm Award for *Invisible Man*.

1954
Rockefeller Foundation Award.

1955

Ellison receives Prix de Rome Fellowship, moves to Rome and begins work on second novel.

1962–1964

Visiting professor at Rutgers University.

1964

Shadow and Act published by Random House.

1965

Book Week poll selects *Invisible Man* as the most distinguished post–World War II American novel; "Juneteenth" (from second novel) published; Ellison becomes a charter member of the National Council of the Arts.

1966–1967

Serves on the Carnegie Commission on Educational Television.

1967

Pages of second novel destroyed in fire.

1969

President Johnson confers the Medal of Freedom.

1970

Appointed Albert Schweitzer Professor in Humanities at New York University; receives the Chevalier de l'Ordre des Arts et Lettres from France.

1973

"Cadillac Flambé," from his second novel, is published.

1986

Going to the Territory published by Random House.

1994

Ellison dies in Manhattan on April 16.

1995

The Collected Essays of Ralph Ellison, edited by John Callahan, Ellison's literary executor, is published by Random House (Modern Library).

1996

Flying Home and Other Stories, edited by John Callahan, is published by Random House.

1999

Juneteenth (second novel), edited by John Callahan, is published by Random House.

2000

Trading Twelves: The Selected Letters of Ralph Ellison and Albert Murray, edited by Albert Murray and John Callahan, published by Modern Library.

Jazz States
Ralph Waldo Ellison's Major Chords

The Americans of all nations at any time upon the earth have probably the fullest poetical nature. The United States themselves are essentially the greatest poem. . . . Here is not merely a nation but a teeming nation of nations.
—Walt Whitman, preface to Leaves of Grass (1855)

Jazz Country discusses Ralph Ellison's working assumptions about American culture, jazz, and what he calls "the drama of democracy." It addresses Ellison's jazz background, including his essays and comments about jazz musicians such as Louis Armstrong, Charlie Christian, Duke Ellington, Lester Young, and Charlie Parker, and examines the influence of Duke Ellington and Louis Armstrong upon the writer's personal and artistic inspiration. It highlights the significance of the camaraderie between Ellison and two African American friends and fellow jazz fans — the writer Albert Murray and the painter Romare Bearden. Ellison's relationship to jazz is the book's central theme, but it also touches upon the blues. While learning to play the trumpet, he listened to and imitated the blues singers Ida Cox and Ma Rainey. He writes about various blues and jazz influences upon Mahalia Jackson's gospel singing, and he captures the evocative power of Jimmy Rushing's blues voice. These singers deeply influenced the writer's developing artistic sensibility. Furthermore, Ellison's own study of music taught him something about the art of fiction as he began his transformation from aspiring classical composer to novelist.

Jazz Country also shows how Ellison appropriated jazz techniques in *Invisible Man* (1952) and in his posthumously published second novel, *Juneteenth* (1999). The book's concluding chapter discusses

Ellison and his critics, including Irving Howe, Norman Mailer, Norman Podhoretz, Addison Gayle, Amiri Baraka, and Jerry Watts. Richard Wright and James Baldwin also figure in Ellison's famous exchange with Howe concerning the appropriate role and subjects of African American writers.

Using jazz as the key metaphor, Jazz Country refocuses older interpretations of Ellison by placing jazz in the foreground and by emphasizing, especially as revealed in his essays, the power of Ellison's thought and cultural perceptions. The failure to perceive and to define accurately the subtleties of Ellison's thought and the complex nature of his artistic ambition constitute a significant limitation of previous criticism on him. Few critics, for instance, have thoroughly discussed his essays. Since Ellison was a self-described "custodian of American culture," his major essays, originally published in Shadow and Act (1964) and Going to the Territory (1986) — all anthologized in The Collected Essays of Ralph Ellison (1995) — are significant artifacts in their own right. His essays on various aspects of American culture constitute a gallery of American portraits, including ones on jazz musicians such as Charlie Christian and Charlie Parker, the writers Stephen Crane and Henry James, the artist Romare Bearden, and President Lyndon Johnson. In his autobiographical essays, Ellison paints a complex self-portrait. He writes of himself as a black boy in Oklahoma City, an aspiring musician in Tuskegee, Alabama, a struggling young writer in New York City, then a prizewinning first novelist. We finally see him as an embattled cultural icon and a dedicated writer struggling to complete his second novel, in part the story of Rev. A. Z. Hickman, a jazz trombonist turned preacher.

Perhaps Ellison drew the inspiration for Rev. Hickman from jazzmen he had known. He admired the jazz musicians he knew during his boyhood in Oklahoma City — the guitarist Charlie Christian, the singer Jimmy Rushing, and the many other celebrated musicians who passed through. Asked by Ron Welburn in 1976 about the time when he had first "become conscious of 'improvised music,'" Ellison described people in Oklahoma City "who amused themselves by playing guitars, Jew's harps, kazoos, yukes, mandolins, C Melody saxophones, or performed on combs by vibrating a piece of tissue paper placed against the comb's teeth." He referred to "territorial orchestras" that were "constantly in and out of Oklahoma City." He mentioned Benny Moten, George E. Lee, T. Holder, and Andy Kirk. The bands played the marches of Sousa and others, arrangements of classics, and "novelty numbers" like the "laughing trombone" with its elements of ragtime and jazz. "There was not," Ellison pointed out, "too definite a line drawn between the types of music, at least not in my kid's consciousness." He also heard the Blue Devils, the city's best dance band, which included such notable musicians of the 1920s as Buster Smith, Walter Page, Harry Youngblood, Oran "Hot Lips" Page, Willie Lewis, and Lester Young.[1]

Ellison began playing the trumpet when he was eight, and he listened to and practiced playing "hard-driving blues." His essay "Living with Music" mentions Ma Rainey, Ida Cox, and Clara Smith, "who made regular appearances" in the town. The blues women were inspirational, and Ellison says, "I knew exactly how I wanted my horn to sound." Neighbors asked him to play Ida Cox's "Trouble in Mind Blues." Ellison says, "I'd draw in my breath and do Miss Cox great violence."[2]

Zelia Breaux, one of Ellison's first music teachers, was a leader in the nation's music education movement. Breaux introduced Ellison "to the basic discipline required of the artist," making it possible for him, as he puts it in "Going to the Territory," "to grasp the basic compatibility of the mixture of the classical and vernacular styles which were part of our musical culture."[3] Breaux herself was "an all-around musician," playing trumpet, violin, and piano, though she did not encourage her students to play jazz. But she was also the owner of the local Aldridge Theater (perhaps named in honor of Ira Aldridge, a famous African American Shakespearean actor), which featured various blues singers and was then the only theater owned by blacks in Oklahoma City that presented programs for blacks. Ellison says Breaux brought "all kinds of jazz musicians before the public," among them King Oliver, the trumpeter who had a profound influence on Louis Armstrong.[4]

Jazz musicians were as a group among Ellison's several boyhood heroes. In his introduction to Shadow and Act he writes: "We fabricated our own heroes and ideals catch as catch can, and with an outrageous and irreverent sense of freedom. . . . Gamblers and scholars, jazz musicians and scientists, Negro cowboys and soldiers from the Spanish-American and first world wars, movie stars and stunt men, figures from the Italian Renaissance and literature, both classical and popular, were combined with the special virtues of some local bootlegger, the eloquence of some Negro preacher, the strength and grace of some local athlete, the ruthlessness of some businessman-physician, the elegance in dress and manners of some headwaiter or hotel doorman."[5] Like Whitman's speaker in "Song of Myself," who creates a parade of American types, Ellison dramatizes the cultural richness of his native Oklahoma City.

For Ellison, jazz musicians also definitively personify African American experience. Musicians like Duke Ellington, Louis Armstrong, and Lester Young — who played in Oklahoma during the 1920s and 1930s — inspired Ellison and his boyhood friends: "And we recognized and were proud of our group's own cultural style wherever we discerned it — in jazzmen and prizefighters, ballplayers and tap dancers; in gesture, inflection, intonation, timbre and phrasing. . . . We did not fully understand the cost of the style but recognized within it an affirmation of life beyond all question of our difficulties as Negroes."[6] Ellison consistently calls attention to "an affirmation of life," whether noting how jazz artists did not "compromise their vision" or how their visions inspired dreams of possibility that served as answers and antidotes to racial injustice. Furthermore, he stresses his boyhood pride in "our own group's cultural style." African Americans have, over the centuries, taken an eclectic assortment of cultural strands and woven them into the fabric of their existence. And this process of what Nathan I. Huggins calls "Afro-Americanization" has shaped American culture. Jazz symbolizes the process of Afro-Americanization and is as well one of its marvelous exhibits. It is both African American and American music.[7]

In "Ralph Waldo Ellison: Anthropology, Modernism and Jazz," Berndt Ostendorf makes a similar point: "For Ellison, Jazz represents a working out of an American vernacular, a national style. In fact, for him, all American culture, including baseball, is 'jazz-shaped.' Jazz is an example and chief exhibit for Ellison's conception of a pluralist culture that, as opposed to bounded social and political systems of power, knows no frontiers, whether marked by color or genes."[8]

New York City — with its skyscrapers and multifarious variety of human types — is literally and figuratively "jazz shaped." After leaving Oklahoma City and spending three years studying music at Tuskegee Institute, Ellison arrived in New York City during 1936. He was "dazzled by the lights." He explored Manhattan like an anthropologist: "I listened to diction and noted dress, and searched for attitudes in inflections, carriage, and manners. . . . I crossed Manhattan back and forth from river to river and up, down and around again, from Spuyten Duyvil Creek to the Battery. . . . From the elevated trains I saw my first penthouses with green trees growing atop tall buildings . . . while moving above the teeming streets, and felt a sense of quiet tranquility despite the bang and clatter."[9] His transformation from musician to writer began after meeting Langston Hughes, who, shortly after Ellison's arrival in New York, arranged a meeting with Richard Wright.

At Wright's suggestion, Ellison began writing reviews and short stories. He joined the Federal Writers' Project in 1938 and published his first short story, "Slick Gonna Learn," in 1939.[10] In 1952 Ellison published *Invisible Man*, for which he received the National Book Award. The citation read: "In it [*Invisible Man*] he shows us how invisible we all are to each other. With a positive exuberance of narrative gifts, he has broken away from the conventions and patterns of the 'well-made' novel. Mr. Ellison has the courage to take many literary risks, and he has succeeded with them."[11] First novelists are rarely so successful. Yet despite the achievement of *Invisible Man*, Ellison worried about the craft and function of fiction. Few, if any, American writers after World War II have spoken so consistently and with such compelling authority on the American novel and democracy, or on the relationship between blacks and whites in the shaping of American culture, or on the challenge to the American writer of writing serious fiction for and about such a diverse audience.

Ellison's self-appointed role as custodian and conscience of American culture, his comments calling for artistic standards, and his ongoing faith in the promise of democracy have led, over several decades, to various celebrations of and attacks upon him and his novel. In his introduction to *New Essays on* Invisible Man, Robert O'Meally describes the novel's "ascent toward classic heights": "The National Book Award was only the most prominent prize the novel won. It also received the National Newspaper Publishers' Award (1953) and the *Chicago Defender*'s award as the work symbolizing the best in American democracy" (1953).[12] In 1965, a poll by *Book Week* of two hundred prominent authors, critics, and editors judged *Invisible Man* the most distinguished single work published in the previous twenty years. Saul Bellow, Ellison's friend, was judged the number one writer. But even with just one novel to his credit, Ellison was number six—above Norman Mailer and Ernest Hemingway, numbers seven and eight, respectively.[13]

Yet early assessments of Ellison were not all favorable. And during the 1960s and 1970s, his devotion to the craft and art of fiction inspired frequent criticism from various camps. Some black writers and critics labeled him a conservative. Addison Gayle, a staunch proponent of "black aesthetics," generally praised Invisible Man but denounced the "political beliefs" found there: "The central flaw in the character of the protagonist, that which mars an otherwise superb novel, is to be attributable more to Ellison's political beliefs than to artistic deficiency. . . . Ellison's protagonist chooses death over life, opts for noncreativity instead of creativity, chooses the path of the individual instead of racial unity."[14] Gayle's view is related to Irving Howe's criticism in "Black Boys and Native Sons," in which Howe praises Richard Wright and criticizes both Baldwin and Ellison for failing to follow in Wright's footsteps.[15] (Ellison would respond openly to Howe in his essay "The World and the Jug.")

Ellison's critics and detractors, as well as some of his supporters, rarely seem interested in sorting through the nuances of his thought. He is usually pigeonholed as "conservative" or "integrationist" or "elitist." To be sure, Invisible Man is in many respects a political narrative that dramatizes certain limitations, related to racial matters, of Communist or social thought. In general, it calls into question discrepancies between the rhetoric and the reality of democracy. Even so, as a writer, Ellison defies easy political or social categorization. When Ellison explicitly states that he sees his own writing as a necessary continuation of standards and practices that include the best of European and American literature, his critics usually miss or ignore the artistic assumptions and aspects of his talent that are most original and jazzlike: "And the main perspective through which a writer looks at experience is that provided by literature . . . an accumulation of techniques, insights, instruments, and processes which have been slowly developed over long periods of time. So when I look at my material, I'm not looking at it simply through the concepts of sociology. . . . I look at it through literature; English, French, Spanish, Russian — especially nineteenth-century Russian literature. And Irish literature, Joyce and Yeats. . . . And through the perspective of folklore. When I listen to a folk story I'm looking for what it conceals as well as what it states. I read it with the same fullness of attention I bring to *Finnegans Wake* or *The Sound and the Fury* because I'm eager to discover what it has to say to me personally." [16]

Those of Ellison's critics who charge elitism and, to a lesser degree, those supporters who celebrate him as an arbiter of literary standards do not take into account the range of his literary taste and the spectrum of sources — from Negro folklore to *Finnegans Wake* — that fuel his imagination. They fail also to understand the degree to which Ellison, like a jazz virtuoso, is dedicated to lending form (through "an accumulation of techniques, insights, instruments") to Whitman's description of America in his preface to the 1855 edition of *Leaves of Grass*: "The United States themselves are essentially the greatest poem."

Ellison's ambition for American fiction and poetry is comprehensive and perhaps, in the form that he imagines it, impossible of fulfillment. Yet his ambition, while expansive, is not exclusive in any hierarchical way. He recognizes no absolute distinctions between "high" and "low" or popular culture, despite what his critics suggest. In "Going to the Territory," Ellison uses jazz and Mark Twain's writings as artistic examples that contradict "a supposedly unresolvable conflict between elitist and populist values." He writes: "In a sense jazz, which is an amalgam of past musical styles, may be seen as a rejection of a music which expressed the values of a social elite, but let me say that although jazz musicians are practitioners of a vernacular style, they are also unreconstructed elitists when it comes to maintaining the highest standards of the music which expresses their sense of the American experience." He says that Twain "transformed elements of regional vernacular speech into a medium of uniquely American literary expression" and understood "how to capture that which is essentially American in our folkways and manners." Ellison concludes that "the vernacular process is a way of establishing and discovering our national identity." [17]

Ellison's overall view of American culture seems more radical than conservative. He consistently questions various experts' views on race, culture, and the art of fiction, and he frequently offers his own carefully articulated positions on such matters. Perhaps, given his hidden middle name, we might think of Ralph Waldo Ellison as a radical transcendentalist or metaphysical rebel, for, like his namesake Emerson, Ellison is an independent thinker, an intellectual compelled to commune with his own heart and mind, and forced to pay the high price of public criticism, even scathing denunciation.

He is a radical transcendentalist or metaphysical rebel because he believes in "transcendence," in the possibility for individuals and nations — given a combination of will, imagination, and intelligence — to rise above their immediate circumstances. He is also a steadfast optimist. Yet his optimistic or nationalistic perspective always contains original, radical, even subversive, elements. Ellison dedicated himself to writing about ambiguity, irony, and contradiction in American life. While he often holds forth with Jamesian eloquence on "tradition," "standards," "excellence," "elegance" and "form," he remains acutely aware that art, no less than the nation, is perpetually threatened by "chaos," his label for the negative in general and social disintegration in particular. He is an optimist, but his overall vision may be more accurately described as tragicomic, as he himself describes the fundamental situation of African Americans. For instance, in "Blues People," his essay on the book of the same title by Leroi Jones (Amiri Baraka), he writes: "The blues speak to us simultaneously of the tragic and the comic aspects of the human condition and they express a profound sense of life shared by many Negro Americans precisely because their lives have combined these modes. This has been the heritage of a people who for hundreds of years could not celebrate birth or dignify death and whose need to live despite the dehumanizing pressures of slavery developed an endless capacity for laughing at their painful experiences." [18]

Ellison uses a special vocabulary to emphasize and accent his principal themes. In *Jazz Country*, I call these central themes "major chords" and use words that appear frequently in his writings — *unity, ambiguity, possibility, discipline,* and *transcendence* — to note specific chords. Each major chord has variations, including its implied opposite: *unity,* for instance, is connected to diversity, *possibility* and *transcendence* are related to defeat. One can discern in Ellison's fiction and essays an ongoing dramatization of his recurrent themes.

Ellison speaks of America's "experiment in democracy," an ongoing and definitive process of unexpected developments and changes. He sees human experience in general and American experience in particular as a whole. He often alludes in an old-fashioned way to "the fundamental continuities of humanity." (If, I wager, Ellison were confronted with contemporary assumptions about the limiting, indeed blinding, specificities of particular cultures, he would readily concede the point. But he would add that all humans are somehow bound together by our various responses to the benign indifference of nature itself. And we are bound by situations arising definitively out of the rituals, necessities, and consequences of human nature, whether truth and error, war and peace, or birth, marriage, and death.) His sense of unity in the American cultural context echoes Walt Whitman's rhapsodic adoration of American things and types. The fifty United States, with their diversity of individuals and groups, are to Ellison as to Whitman a source of countless cultural and personal possibilities. We are all one, though many, "unity in the diversity."

Like Henry James, Ellison is keenly aware, in James's phrase, of the "complex fate" of being an American. Ellison focuses on the national dynamics of being one and yet many and the distinctly American ironies and contradictions to which such circumstances inexorably lead. Chief among the ironies is the ambiguous role African Americans have played in the history and cultural development of the nation. Ellison states: "On the moral level I propose that we view the whole of American life as a drama acted out upon the body of a Negro giant, who, lying trussed up like Gulliver, forms the stage and scene upon which and within which the action unfolds."[19] Put another way, while African Americans have often been segregated and excluded, they have remained at the center of the country's ongoing debate about democracy and freedom. Ellison also stresses the "freedom" African Americans have achieved in spite of segregation and discrimination. He says in "An Extravagance of Laughter": "A broad freedom of expression within restrictions could be heard in jazz and seen in sports, and that freedom was made movingly manifest in religious worship."[20]

Unity and ambiguity together create what Ellison calls possibility, the potential to achieve certain personal or national goals, given the demographics, democratic beliefs, and numerous opportunities the United States offers. Possibility is determined by democratic chance and the many ways it provides to explore, exploit, and realize one's individual talents and dreams. To Ellison, possibility also suggests something in a larger cultural sense. There is a special American energy, a collective belief in the promise of democracy and its freedom. And there is a concomitant belief in American initiative and American will. Possibility can rarely be realized without discipline, the necessary price individuals, artists, and nations must pay for the achievement of transcendent meaning. *Discipline* at its best leads to *transcendence* — the process whereby individuals, artists, or nations, as Ellison puts it, "reduce the chaos of living to form." [21]

Ellison celebrates the cultural variety within the United States — the seemingly random blending of styles, values, and ways of living. The definitive element that is "American" is the nation's improvisational process of cultural development. In "The Little Man at Chehaw Station" he writes: "The Pilgrims began by appropriating the agricultural, military, and meteorological lore of the Indians — including much of their terminology. The Africans, thrown together from numerous ravaged tribes, took up the English language and the biblical legends of the ancient Hebrews and were 'Americanizing' themselves long before the American Revolution. They also had imposed upon them a goodly portion of European chromosomes, and thereby 'inherited' both an immunity to certain European diseases and a complexity of bloodlines and physical characteristics." [22]

Ellison's descriptions of various American blendings and appropriations constitute his version of the melting pot. He strives to mimic the hodgepodge nature of America, its "process of apparently random synthesis," by providing his own inventory list of elements — including law, language, music, religion, sports — that were forever altered. He later refers to "the unconscious logic of the democratic process" and perceives, in the process of "improvising" a "precious" American freedom, "the possibility of enriching the individual self by . . . pragmatic and opportunistic appropriations." [23] In an essay published in *Time* called "What America Would Be Like without Blacks," Ellison criticizes Daniel Patrick Moynihan for insisting that "the American melting pot didn't melt because our white ethnic groups have resisted all assimilative forces that appear to threaten their identities." "The problem here," Ellison writes, "is that few Americans know who and what they really are. That is why few of these groups — or at least few of the children of these groups — have been able to resist the movies, television, baseball, jazz, football, drum-majoretting, rock, comic strips, radio commercials, soap operas, book clubs, slang, or any of a thousand other expressions and carriers of our pluralistic and easily available popular culture. . . . On this level the melting pot did indeed melt, creating such deceptive metamorphoses and blending of identities, values, and life-styles that most American whites are culturally part Negro American without even realizing it." [24]

Thus Ellison gives African Americans a definitive role in the shaping of American experience. He concludes that "without the presence of the Negro," America as we know it would not exist: "Without the presence of Negro American style, our jokes, our tall tales, even our sports would be lacking in the sudden turns, the shocks, the swift changes of pace (all jazz-shaped) that serve to remind us that the world is ever unexplored, and that while a complete mastery of life is mere illusion, the real secret of the game is to make life swing." [25]

In an interview conducted by the writer John Hersey during the 1970s, Ellison said regarding the ambiguous position of African Americans in the United States: "Our social mobility was strictly and violently limited, and in a way that neither our Christianity nor beliefs in the Constitution could change. As the sociologists say, we were indeed disadvantaged, both by law and by custom. Yet our actual position was ambiguous, for although we were outside the social compact, we were existentially right in the middle of the social drama. I mean that as servants we were right in the bedroom, so to speak." [26]

Although Ellison sees American cultural connections and encounters as generally positive, he remains keenly attuned to the inevitability of cultural clashes. In "The Little Man at Chehaw Station," he agrees that the melting pot melts but notes that it creates an ongoing state of unease and contestation. While insisting on the existence of unity in the diversity of American cultural heritage, he says that it is paradoxically American to refuse to see such unity: "So perhaps we shy away from confronting our cultural wholeness because it offers no easily recognizable points of rest, no facile certainties as to who, what or where (culturally or historically) we are. Instead, the whole is always in cacophonic motion. Constantly changing its mode, it appears as a vortex of discordant ways of living and tastes, values and traditions, a whirlpool of odds and ends in which the past courses in uneasy juxtaposition with those bright futuristic principles and promises to which we, as a nation, are politically committed. . . . Deep down, the American condition is a state of unease." [27]

Unlike the critics of the melting pot, Ellison looks beyond "a vortex of discordant ways of living," and sees something definitive and unifying. He believes that there are abundant opportunities found in a national state of cultural flux—chances for individual or collective invention and metamorphosis. He sees it as characteristically American to feel uneasy, perhaps even distrustful, about democratic harmony. In "The Novel as a Function of Democracy," he describes a uniquely American "mystery": "There is a mystery in this country because . . . we wear the same clothing; we listen to the same television programs; we worship the same God; we read the same textbooks; we have the same heroes in sports, in politics, in music. We are at once very, very unified, and at the same time, diversified. On many, many levels we don't know who we are, and there are always moments of confrontation where we meet as absolute strangers."[28]

But even absolute strangers may come to share experiences and eventually know each other. He does not view the national "state of unease" as a final or static situation. Democracy's process of give-and-take, its clash of styles, languages, interests, its battles of clout and will are what Ellison often refers to as "the drama of democracy." The U.S. Constitution guides the dramatic process of democracy: "For I look upon the Constitution as the still-vital covenant by which Americans of diverse backgrounds, religions, races, and interests are bound. . . . The Constitution is a script by which we seek to act out the drama of democracy and the stage upon which we enact our roles."[29]

This complex American drama unfolds as diverse groups seek authority and validation as Americans on a common stage and "the terrain upon which we [Americans] struggle." The "terrain" is formed by the ideas that "draw their power from the Declaration of Independence, the Constitution, and the Bill of Rights." Yet such ideas are both unifying and divisive: "But indeed it is in the name of these same principles that we ceaselessly contend, affirming our ideals even as we do them violence."[30] "Indeed," Ellison says elsewhere, "a battle-royal conflict of interests appears to be basic to our conception of freedom, and the drama of democracy proceeds through a warfare of words and symbolic actions by which we seek to advance our private interests while resolving our political differences."[31]

One aspect of the democratic drama is less contentious. Ellison sometimes refers to the "unexpectedness" of American life. He tells anecdotes and writes about individuals and situations that seem completely incongruous. He explains that America's cultural and class fluidity often leads to such incongruities, but so does a supposedly fixed hierarchical system like racial segregation. Ellison sometimes uses his personal experience to emphasize what he calls the "ironies" of segregation.

For example, he begins "The Little Man at Chehaw Station" with an apparently straightforward account of a day in his life as a music student at Tuskegee Institute. Tuskegee, headed by Booker T. Washington in 1881, was (in 1933–36 when Ellison attended) a small agricultural and technical college for blacks located in rural Alabama. The Chehaw Station train depot was a short distance from the college. But Chehaw Station and Tuskegee are merely Ellison's backdrop, the setting of a revealing American scene. As Ellison recalls the day, he had, dressed in a tuxedo, given a formal trumpet recital for the faculty members of Tuskegee's Department of Music. At the recital's end, he received negative criticism from the music faculty because, he says, he substituted "a certain skill of lips and fingers for the intelligent structuring of emotion that was demanded in performing the music."[32]

One of the faculty members, Miss Hazel Harrison, was an accomplished concert pianist. Ellison writes: "Miss Harrison had been one of Ferruccio Busoni's prize pupils, had lived (until the rise of Hitler had driven her back to a U.S.A. that was not yet ready to recognize her talents) in Busoni's home in Berlin, and was a friend of such masters as Egon Petri, Percy Grainger and Sergei Prokofiev." By presenting Miss Harrison's musical pedigree, Ellison clearly intends to suggest a ritual of initiation into the elite ranks of classical music culture. The scene is heightened by Tuskegee's rural and segregated situation. Yet Ellison, then an aspiring composer of symphonies, was being held, as though he were at Julliard, to the highest standards of classical musicianship. Miss Harrison tells Ellison: "You must *always* play your best, even if it's only in the waiting room at Chehaw Station, because in this country there'll always be a little man hidden behind the stove . . . the little man whom you don't expect, and he'll know the *music*, and the *tradition*, and the standards of musicianship required for whatever you set out to perform."[33]

Miss Harrison's comment stands as a parable about high standards as well as the unknown audiences all true artists perpetually face. She personifies one of Ellison's major points. He often calls attention to the "unstructured possibilities of culture in a pluralistic society," and the sometimes capricious nature of cultural transmission and transformation within the United States. He says that "there is no reliable sociology of the dispersal of ideas, styles, or tastes in this turbulent American society." Miss Harrison's presence in both Berlin and Alabama was proof of the unexpected direction of various ideas and tastes. The very nature of the United States — its dedication to speed, mobility, and progress; its glamorous technology — all combine to create a culture defined, as Ellison puts it, by "an incalculable scale of possibilities for self-creation." Ellison describes this definitive cultural phenomenon as "a climate of free-floating sensibility . . . in which certain assertions of personality, formerly the prerogative of high social rank, have become the privilege of the anonymous and the lowly." [34]

He notes "the frequency and wide dispersal of individuals" who avail themselves of "many of the finest products of the arts and intellect — products that are so abundantly available in the form of books, graphics, recordings, and pictorial reproductions as to escape sustained attempts at critical evaluation." [35] From Ellison's perspective such "anonymous" individuals often exercise the American freedom of using whatever resources they find to make themselves up, to create identities of parts taken from here and there. These individuals are human exhibits of democratic culture at work, walking personifications of the cultural complexity of the United States.

Discipline, another Ellisonian major chord, surfaces repeatedly in Ellison's discussions of writing, music, African American life, and the American nation. As Ellison sees it, a writer must first develop the discipline to master literary technique. This process involves something more than being able, for example, to write a convincing story. It involves the particular writer's whole way of seeing and knowing. He celebrates jazz musicians such as Louis Armstrong and Duke Ellington as exemplary figures having the discipline required to achieve and sustain virtuosity. He writes of the discipline African Americans have relied upon as a psychological antidote to prejudice. For instance, in "The World and the Jug," his reply to the critic Irving Howe, Ellison concludes that African Americans are, "in a limited way," their "own creation": "For even as his life toughens the Negro, even as it brutalizes him, sensitizes him, dulls him, goads him to anger, moves him to irony, sometimes fracturing and sometimes affirming his hopes; even as it shapes his attitudes toward family, sex, love, religion . . . it conditions him to deal with his life and with himself. Because it is his life and no mere abstraction in someone's head. . . . He is a product of the interaction between his racial predicament, his individual will and the broader American cultural freedom in which he finds his ambiguous existence."[36] And he speaks of the discipline the nation must acquire in order to move toward social equality. If African American reality is "ambiguous," so is that of the nation at large, precisely because African Americans have played such a definitive role in the shaping of its culture. Ellison believes that the discipline and goodwill required to understand the complex fate of being an American are inextricably linked to an accurate perception of the impact of African Americans on American reality. Only with such a perception can the nation achieve transcendent moments of democratic possibility.

Transcendence is arguably the most significant among Ellison's major chords or concepts. Transcendence involves the daunting process, in his words, of "reducing the chaos of living to form." He often points out how African Americans, given their discipline, have transcended the brutal reality of racial discrimination and violence. He frequently calls attention to the inextricable nature of "the marvelous and the terrible," his term for the positive and negative aspects of African American culture. In "A Very Stern Discipline," Ellison speaks of that "heroic" aspect of African American experience that goes beyond the consequences of racial discrimination: "I do not find it a strain to point to the heroic component of our [African American] experience. . . . I am not denying the negative things which have happened to us and which continue to happen, but I am compelled to reject all condescending, narrowly paternalistic interpretations of Negro American life and personality from whatever quarters they come, whether white or Negro. Such interpretations would take the negative details of our existence and make them the whole of our life and personality."[37]

Ellison also believed that through stern discipline a writer can evoke a sense of transcendent possibility. In "The Art of Fiction" (1955), a revealing early interview, the stance Ellison took is the position he maintained for the remaining thirty-nine years of his life. The characteristic elements of Ellison's vision are clear. He pays homage to Joyce, Stein, Dostoevsky, Hemingway, and Malraux, a few of his idols. He discusses the significance of Negro folklore and alludes to the importance of jazz as an art form. He looks back to the nineteenth century as the golden age of American literature, calling Melville's *Moby-Dick* and Twain's *Adventures of Huckleberry Finn* "our two great nineteenth-century novels." Ellison continues in that tradition:

"I feel that with my decision to devote myself to the novel I took on one of the responsibilities inherited by those who practice the craft in the United States: that of describing for all that fragment of the huge diverse American experience which I know best, and which offers me the possibility of contributing not only to the growth of the literature but to the shaping of the culture as I should like it to be. The American novel is in this sense a conquest of the frontier; as it describes experience, it creates it."[38]

Ellison makes similar statements on various occasions at different stages of his career. In the beginning of "Hidden Name and Complex Fate" (1964), he speaks of how individual writers have used their imaginations to give violence and injustice a coherent and figurative meaning: "It is a matter of outrageous irony, perhaps, but in literature, the great social clashes of history, no less than the painful experiences of the individual, are secondary to the meaning they take on through the skill, talent, imagination and personal vision of the writer who transforms them into art. Here they are reduced to more manageable proportions; here they are imbued with humane values; here injustice and catastrophe become less important in themselves than what the writer makes of them."[39]

In his introduction to the thirtieth anniversary edition of *Invisible Man* (1982), Ellison again trumpets his major chords about unity in diversity, the connection between fiction and democracy in the United States, and the necessity of the artist to reveal "transcendent truths": "So if the ideal of achieving a true political equality eludes us in reality — as it continues to do — there is still available that fictional *vision* of an ideal democracy in which the actual combines with the ideal and gives us representations of a state of things in which the highly placed and the lowly, the black and the white, the Northerner and the Southerner, the native-born and the immigrant are combined to tell us of transcendent truths and possibilities such as those discovered when Mark Twain set Huck and Jim afloat on the raft. Which suggested to me that a novel could be fashioned as a raft of hope, perception and entertainment that might help keep us afloat as we tried to negotiate the snags and whirlpools that mark our nation's vacillating course toward and away from the democratic ideal."[40]

Jazz Essays
Ellison on Charlie Christian, Jimmy Rushing, Mahalia Jackson, and Lester Young

. . . Pat Marino. He was the big shocker for me when I found out he was only seventeen years old and I saw what he could accomplish. He was one of the first guitars I saw when I came to New York, and he had no big name. He was like myself. He had just come to New York to work. . . . And I walked into the nightclub. It was in the middle of Harlem, and here was a young Sicilian boy with his sunglasses on, standing up reading the music on the floor. . . . And, when they let him take a solo, I mean, he lifted that song up off the ground and turned it every way but loose. And I said, "Boy, this is an example of what's going on in New York City! I better hurry up and get out of here." I didn't realize that he was really an exception. All the other players who had big names at that time, I would watch them. . . . I would steal a few things off of everybody and turn it around and make it comfortable for me. And pretty soon it all started coming together.
— George Benson, in Talking Jazz by Ben Sidran

The Solo Voice of Charlie Christian's Guitar

In his introduction to *Shadow and Act* (1964), Ralph Ellison explains how growing up in Oklahoma City inspired him to become a "renaissance man." He maintains that he cannot provide a precise genealogy of his ideal renaissance man, but assures us that he "shared it with a half dozen of my Negro friends." Perhaps the source was a "transplanted New Englander," "some book," or "idealistic Negro teacher." He consistently holds up his native Oklahoma to prove a point concerning both his own background and the country as a whole: "One thing is certain, ours was a chaotic community, still characterized by frontier attitudes and by that strange mixture of the naive and sophisticated . . . that mixture which often affords the minds of the young who grow up in the far provinces such wide and unstructured latitude, and which encourages the individual's imagination — up to the moment 'reality' closes in upon him — to range widely and, sometimes, even to soar." [1]

To Ellison, the Oklahoma jazz musician personifies the ideal renaissance man. He writes: "We hear the effects of this [attitude] in the southwestern jazz of the thirties, that joint creation of artistically free and exuberantly creative adventurers, of artists who had stumbled upon the freedom lying within the restrictions of their musical tradition as within the limitations of their social background, and who in their own unconscious way have set an example for any Americans, Negro or white, who would find themselves in the arts." Such musicians are renaissance men in the sense that they construct or invent themselves, just as they — through instinct and practice — become jazz virtuosos. They succeed both because of and in spite of racial prejudice or "the limitations of their social backgrounds." Ellison's phrase, "freedom lying within restrictions," crystallizes the musicians' relationship to their developing art form no less than to their exploitation of the ambiguities of their social situation. Put another way, they invent forms and expressions of both personal and artistic freedom. They improvise as they go along. Given their dedication to jazz, Ellison says, "whatever others thought or felt, this was their own powerful statement, and only nonmusical assaults upon their artistic integrity . . . were able to compromise their vision." [2]

The jazzmen's music possessed unimpeachable authority. Nevertheless, given various laws and customs, the musicians were sometimes subjected to racial prejudice and discrimination. But they did not view themselves as victims. Neither did boys like Ellison. Ellison says that he and his boyhood friends absorbed, as if by cultural osmosis, certain jazzmen's renaissance ideals of freedom and personal fulfillment. The jazz guitarist Charlie Christian was one of these friends. Although Christian died young, Ellison saw his life as an example of American possibility. In "The Charlie Christian Story," an article he wrote in 1958 for the Saturday Review, Ellison also corrects certain mistaken notions about jazz and jazz musicians and begins to clarify the history and significance of jazz. Ellison had (in 1955) already written "Living with Music," a short essay published in High

Fidelity. He had also published "Richard Wright's Blues," a review of Wright's autobiography *Black Boy* (1945) and one of his two blues-related articles (the other is a review essay on *Blues People*, 1964). He later published five other essays on jazz artists and jazz-related themes for *Saturday Review* and *Esquire*. His last published jazz-related article, "Homage to Duke Ellington," was written in 1969 for the *Washington Star* on the occasion of the composer's seventieth birthday. Themes developed in the later articles, such as the Ellington homage, are foreshadowed in Ellison's first articles, "Living with Music" and "The Charlie Christian Story." Occasional pieces on musicians or jazz clubs, like New York's Minton's Playhouse, set forth his ideas about the workings of jazz.

Ellison's essays are some of the first to provide a thorough cultural analysis of the origins and aesthetics of jazz. But several black writers and critics of an earlier era had commented presciently on the music. Alain Locke, a Harvard- and Oxford-trained philosopher and the first African American Rhodes Scholar, published his seminal anthology of essays, fiction, and poetry by and about Negroes, *The New Negro*, in 1925. He included an essay by J. A. Rogers (a notable journalist who wrote for the *Messenger* and the *Amsterdam News*) called "Jazz at Home." In it Rogers says that jazz "ranks with the movie and the dollar as a foremost exponent of American modernism." "The true spirit of jazz," Rogers writes: "is a joyous revolt from convention, custom, authority, boredom, even sorrow — from everything that would confine the soul of man and hinder its riding free on the air. . . . And that is why it has been such a balm for modern ennui, and has become a safety valve for modern machine-ridden and convention-bound society. It is a revolt of the emotions against repression." [3]

In his later book, *The Negro and His Music* (1938), Locke devotes three of thirteen chapters to jazz. Locke's work anticipates some of Ellison's own ideas. For example, in his chapter "From Jazz to Jazz Classics: 1926–1936," Locke writes: "Much of the musical superiority and force of jazz comes from the fact that the men who play it create it. In the typical Negro jazz band, the musicians compose as a group under the leadership of a conductor who is also a composer or at least an arranger. The music comes alive from the activity of the group, like folk music originally does, instead of being a mere piece of musical execution." [4]

Ellison read Locke's work and was influenced by it. But when Ellison began publishing his essays, he was nonetheless a pioneer of American cultural studies. He criticized early jazz reviewers, critics, and historians, and corrected various simplistic interpretations of jazz: "We know much of jazz as entertainment, but a mere handful of clichés constitutes our knowledge of jazz as experience. It is this which leads to the notion that jazz was invented in a particular house of ill fame by 'Jelly Roll' Morton, who admitted the crime himself; that swing was invented by Goodman about 1935; that T. Monk, K. Clarke, and J. B. 'D' Gillespie invented 'progressive' jazz at Minton's Playhouse in Harlem about 1941." He addresses, for example, the apparent mystery surrounding certain jazz musicians' backgrounds. Those from the South, the Southwest, and the Midwest, where, as he explains, "jazz is part of a total way of life" are sometimes presented as though they found their horns and voices in the big cities: "The jazz artist who becomes nationally known is written about as though he came into existence only upon his arrival in New York. . . . Thus we are left with an impression of mysterious rootlessness."[5] He demonstrates how misleading such characterizations can be when he discusses Charlie Christian's background. And he repeatedly takes issue with those journalists and sociologists who interpret American culture in terms of reductive categories — "culturally disadvantaged," "culturally deprived," and "culturally marginal."

"The Charlie Christian Story" is a pointed example of Ellison's overall vision of American culture. Christian stands in as Ellison's alter ego; the guitarist, too, is a representative of the "wild" state of Oklahoma. He is an African American from an impoverished background, and a musical genius. Christian's life, like that of other jazz musicians, is a Horatio Alger story but one with a tragic end. "The wooden tenement in which he grew up," Ellison writes, "was full of poverty, crime and sickness. It was alive and exciting, and I enjoyed visiting there, for the people both lived and sang the blues." Although Christian "spent much of his life in a slum in which all the forms of disintegration attending the urbanization of rural Negroes ran riot," Ellison points out that Christian's family circumstances did not negate rich musical experience. Ellison tells us: "Before Charlie was big enough to handle a guitar himself he served as a guide for his father, a blind guitarist and singer. Later he joined with his father, his brothers Clarence and Edward (an arranger, pianist, violinist and performer on the string bass and tuba), and made his contribution to the family income by strolling with them through the white middle-class sections of Oklahoma City, where they played serenades on request. Their repertory included the light classics as well as the blues." At the Frederick Douglass School, the public school Ellison and Christian attended, "Harmony was taught from the ninth through the twelfth grade" and there was an "extensive and compulsory music-appreciation" program.[6]

Ellison demonstrates convincingly how Oklahoma City — though far removed from Harlem and its famed Harlem Renaissance — was a wonderful place for any boy dreaming of becoming a jazz musician. In his essay "Homage to Duke Ellington," he tells of Ellington's bringing his "great orchestra" to Oklahoma City. Ellison, along with Christian, saw the orchestra's glamorous performance, heard Ellington's fascinating rhythms and the singing of Ivy Anderson and Ethel Waters. Christian also heard Lester Young, the tenor saxophonist who became the famous "Prez." "The most stimulating influence upon Christian," Ellison notes, was a "tall, intense young musician who arrived in Oklahoma City sometime in 1929 and who, with his heavy white sweater and blue stocking cap and up-and-out-thrust silver saxophone, left absolutely no reed player and few young players of any instrument unstirred by wild, excitingly original flights of his imagination." Young "upset the entire Negro section of the town."[7]

"The Charlie Christian Story" hints at some of the themes Ellison spells out five years later in "The World and the Jug" (1963), his controversial exchange with Irving Howe. Ellison makes clear that he, like Christian, found in Oklahoma City inspiring models and a nurturing environment despite the grim reality emphasized by certain journalists and sociologists. He and Christian escaped into music and literature. They were not alone even in segregated Oklahoma City. Other black children could also read, play music and sports, and imagine worlds elsewhere.

"The Charlie Christian Story" also reveals Ellison's expertise as a jazz critic. He points out that Christian escaped a "tension" some early jazzmen faced: "He [the early player of jazz] feels a tension between his desire to master the classical style of playing and his compulsion to express those sounds which form a musical definition of

Negro American music. In early jazz these sounds found their fullest expression in the timbre of the blues voice, and the use of mutes, water glasses and derbies on the bells of their horns arose out of an attempt to imitate this sound." Younger musicians, of the 1930s, seeking recognition beyond their local black communities, tried to cast aside "those nonmusical features which came into jazz from the minstrel tradition." Ellison is keenly aware of how musicians such as the Mills Brothers (who duplicated with their voices the sounds of certain musical instruments) and Louis Armstrong exploited the minstrel tradition while creating technical innovations. But the younger musicians' negative response to the minstrel tradition, in addition to the tension between classical techniques and the eclectic innovations of early jazz, led, Ellison believes, "to many of the technical discoveries of jazz."[8]

Some of the advances were in accordance with the inherent aesthetics, the "cruel contradiction," implicit in the jazz tradition. Ellison sees a revealing relationship between the musician's sense of his own performance and that of the group: "For true jazz is an art of individual assertion within and against the group. Each true jazz moment (as distinct from the uninspired commercial performance) springs from a contest in which each artist challenges all the rest; each solo flight, or improvisation, represents (like the successive canvases of a painter) a definition of his identity: as individual, as member of the collectivity and as a link in the chain of tradition. Thus, because jazz finds its very life in an endless improvisation upon traditional materials, the jazzman must lose his identity even as he finds it."[9]

Reducing the Chaos of Living to Form: The Affirmative Voices of Jimmy Rushing and Mahalia Jackson

"The Charlie Christian Story" is merely one example of Ellison's ongoing commentary on the relationship between jazz and American culture. Ellison's other essays seek to rescue the jazz tradition from shallow mythology, inaccuracies, and stereotypes. He sees in jazz culture an affirmation of life beyond the jazz musicians' expression of the inherent dignity of true style. In "Living with Music," Ellison says that "the driving motivation" of jazz artists is "neither fame nor money": "I had learned too that the end of all this discipline and technical mastery was the desire to express an affirmative way of life through its musical tradition . . . when they expressed their attitude toward the world it was with a fluid style that reduced the chaos of living to form."[10] The lives and music of Christian and Jimmy Rushing simultaneously represent the transformative power of jazz and the definitively American milieu which gave rise to their complex fates.

Ellison's good friend Jimmy Rushing was already an Oklahoma City celebrity during Ellison's boyhood. Rushing, who eventually became nationally known as the lead singer for Count Basie's band, had, like Ellison, studied music at Douglass High School. For a time, Rushing was also a member of Oklahoma's most notable dance band of that era, the Blue Devils. In "That Same Pain, That Same Pleasure," Ellison says: "I knew Jimmy Rushing, the blues singer, who then was not quite the hero . . . he is today after years of popular success. But for us, even when he was a very young man, . . . Jimmy represented, gave voice to, something which was very affirming of Negro life, feelings which you really couldn't put into words."[11] Rushing was also a colorful character. He was a short man whose girth, increasing with his age, led to his being known as "Mr. Five by Five," the title of his most popular recording.

In his homage "Remembering Jimmy," Ellison celebrates Rushing's vocal talent and the cultural significance of his singing. In Rushing's voice, he hears a sound that recalls memories of his own early life: "On dance nights, when you stood on the rise of the school grounds two blocks to the east, you could hear it jetting from the dance hall like a blue flame in the dark; now soaring high above the trumpets and trombones, now skimming the froth of reeds and rhythms as it called some woman's anguished name." But Rushing sang about something larger than his own personal circumstances, something beyond the confines of Oklahoma City: "For Jimmy Rushing was not simply a local entertainer, he expressed a value, an attitude about the world for which our lives afforded no other definition. We had a Negro church and a segregated school, a few lodges and fraternal organizations, and beyond these there was all the great white world. . . . Yet there was an optimism within the Negro community and a sense of possibility which, despite our awareness of limitation (dramatized so brutally in the Tulsa riot of 1921), transcended all of this; and it was this rock-bottom sense of reality, coupled with our sense of the possibility of rising above it, which sounded in Rushing's voice."[12]

Beyond the Negro church and the segregated schools, Ellison says, "jazz and public jazz dance was a third institution in our lives, and a vital one; and though Jimmy was far from being a preacher, he was, as official floor manager or master-of-the-dance at Slaughter's Hall, the leader of a public rite." [13] His characterization of Rushing as a leader of a "public rite" suggests a secular priest; he notices in the singer's performance a combination of the sacred and the secular that is reflective of African American life in general.

The Negro church was hardly free of the cultural power and technical influence of jazz. When, for instance, Ellison describes the effects of Mahalia Jackson's gospel singing, he hears a similar "affirmation" of black communal values. He also hears in her voice certain technical appropriations from the jazz world. Ellison does not use the words "value," "attitude," or "optimism" to explain the significance of her voice, but he refers to "the world which Mahalia summons up, . . . the spiritual reality which infuses her songs." She "sings within the heart of the congregation as its own voice of faith." Nor does he view her singing as mere entertainment; the church, not the concert stage, is the more appropriate venue for her phenomenal voice: "Here [within the church] it could be seen that the true function of her singing is not simply to entertain, but to prepare the congregation for the minister's message, to make it receptive to the spirit and, with effects of voice and rhythm, to evoke a shared community of experience." [14]

For Ellison, the black church was Jackson's conservatory. He suggests that Mahalia Jackson spent years honing her talent, and specifies the various techniques and aspects of voice that a singer of Jackson's authority must master. He describes how she appropriated jazz techniques and how certain jazz artists were influenced in turn by the art of gospel singing: "It is an art which depends upon the employment of the full expressive resources of the human voice — from the rough growls employed by blues singers, . . . to the gut tones, which remind us of where the jazz trombone found its human source." "It is most eclectic," Ellison notes, "in its use of other musical idioms; indeed, it borrows any effect which will aid in the arousing and control of emotion. Especially is it free in its use of the effects of jazz; its tempos (with the characteristic economy of Negro expression it shares a common rhythmic and harmonic base with jazz) are taken along with its intonations, and, in ensemble singing, its orchestral voicing." [15]

The drummer Max Roach explicitly characterizes the role of the black church as a conservatory: "To develop the kind of quality Mahalia Jackson developed as a singer takes a lot of time and training. Black people come up in the church at 5, 6, 7, 8 years old. Instead of playing or singing a piece at graduation to show what you have learned the four years you have been in the conservatory, there is, instead, the way a Mahalia Jackson or an Aretha Franklin has developed and demonstrates ability. It is a much stronger form because they have to sing before a group of people and either make somebody cry or jump up and shout for joy." [16]

To evoke such emotions, to create empathetic responses, whether tears of sadness or shouts of joy, the singers sometimes borrow techniques from jazz. Jazz singers also exploit the familiar ritualistic practices of the church. Like Mahalia Jackson, Rushing, too, seeks to evoke, as Ellison puts it, "a shared community of experience" even in the dance hall: "It was when Jimmy's voice began to soar with the spirit of the blues that the dancers — and the musicians — achieved that feeling of communion which was the true meaning of the public jazz dance. The blues, the singer, the band and the dancers formed the vital whole of jazz as an institutional form, and even today neither part is quite complete without the rest." [17] Ellison adds another dimension to his definition of "true jazz" or the "true jazz moment." The jazzman must also achieve an evocation of "soul," a transformative and transcendent sense of being "reborn," a uniquely expressive personality.

Charlie Christian and the
Influence of Lester Young

In "The Charlie Christian Story," Ellison calls for bringing "more serious critical intelligence to this branch [jazz] of our national culture." Ellison's own criticism and essays, his cultural contextualization of jazz and jazz musicians, goes beyond that of many jazz critics. When, for example, Ellison considers how Christian expanded jazz, he concludes: "Starting long before he was aware of his mission, . . . he taught himself how to voice the guitar as a solo instrument, a development made possible through the perfecting of the electronically amplified instrument. . . . With Christian the guitar found its jazz voice." [18]

Mark Gridley echoes Ellison's assessment of Christian's influence.

Gridley notes that Christian and another guitarist, Django Rein-hardt, put the guitar solo on a par with solos on piano and horn. "Charlie Christian mastered what was then the almost unexplored world of electric guitar," Gridley writes. "His long, swinging, single-note-at-a-time lines gave solo guitar the stature of a jazz horn. Some of his phrasing had the fluid swing and the freshness of tenor saxophonist Lester Young. Christian is cited as an influence by almost all modern jazz guitarists who matured before the jazz-rock era. His style provided the foundation for that of Wes Montgomery, who was the single most influential jazz guitarist of the 1960s. This extended Christian's impact long past the 1940s and well into the 1980s."[19] Gridley, like Ellison, stresses the influence of Lester Young and in an indirect manner confirms Ellison's general observation about the relationships among individual jazz musicians to players who precede and follow them. Perhaps Ellison, like Gridley, had Wes Montgomery in mind when he wrote of Christian's wide-ranging influence: "With his entry into jazz circles his musical intelligence was able to exert influence upon his peers and to affect the course of the future development of jazz."[20]

Christian's innovative and technical ability to "voice the guitar as a solo instrument" is directly related to Lester Young's early influence on the young guitarist. Ellison and Gridley highlight the connection between the two musicians. Ellison calls Lester Young "the most stimulating influence upon Christian," and Gridley concludes that Christian's phrasing possesses Young's "fluid swing and freshness." Commenting on Young as an influential musician, Gridley refers to the saxophonist's "voice," his talent at deceptively easy melodic presentation: "He possessed the virtue of deliberate restraint. He could pace a solo so well that it seemed an integral part of the written arrangement. His gift for inventing new, easily singable melodies while he improvised is unsurpassed in jazz history."[21]

Benny Green, a jazz musician and critic, also provides a compelling description of how Young played and why his style was so influential. Young's technical advances — his use of "false" or alternative fingering to "obtain an effect of two or . . . three densities of sound on the same note" only begins to suggest the nature of his talent. Perhaps Christian, like Green, saw and heard something beyond the technical that had an awe-inspiring quality. The "uncanny" aspect of Young's performance was arguably the source of Christian's inspiration to find the guitar's solo voice. "There are moments,"

Green observes, "when all human agency seems to have evaporated . . . there seems to be not a man but a spirit behind the solos. . . . No breath seems to be drawn and no embouchure to be controlling the mouthpiece. . . . Lester seems to have disappeared inside his [saxophone] and become a diabolic extension of the keys." [22] While Christian, by all accounts, lacked Young's personal charisma and style — his porkpie hat, his out-thrust horn — discussions of his life and music tend to follow the outline in Ellison's "Charlie Christian Story." Critics praise Christian for his original and influential music and present his life as a magical, though tragic, American success story.

In *The History of Jazz*, Ted Gioia, another jazz musician and critic, describes Christian's playing, his "dancing triplets and swinging sixteenth notes," and later cites Ellison. Gioia nonetheless provides biographical details for Christian that Ellison does not. Christian got his great American chance to rise from the obscurity of Oklahoma City by auditioning for Benny Goodman. Ellison briefly hints at the matter at the beginning of "The Charlie Christian Story," noting that Christian who, unlike others "whose reputations are limited to a radius of a few hundred miles," was a huge success. Ellison then refers to Christian's "brief, spectacular career with the Benny Goodman Sextet" and concludes: "Had he not come from Oklahoma City in 1939 at the instigation of John Hammond, he might have shared the fate of many we knew in the period when Christian was growing up." [23] In short, "The Charlie Christian Story" represents Ellison's dramatization of jazz as representing American ideas and ideals. The guitarist's success and misfortune give resonance to the opening sentences in Ellison's essay: "Jazz, like the country which gave it birth, is fecund in its inventiveness, swift and traumatic in its developments and terribly wasteful of its resources. It is an orgiastic art which demands great physical stamina of its practitioners, and many of its most talented creators die young." [24]

Soul Brothers Charlie Christian and Benny Goodman: Jazz, Race, and Cultural Exchange

Ellison comments repeatedly that in the United States the ability to perceive the richness and complexity of the American cultural exchange is often blunted by racial categorization. While interviewing Ellison in 1976, Ron Welburn refers to the influence on saxophonists

Coleman Hawkins and Lester Young of white musicians like Frankie Trumbauer, and asks Ellison: "Isn't the impetus for this jazz improvisory style something that sprang from Afro-American imaginative genius?" Ellison replies: "This argument about who did what and who influenced whom imposes racial considerations which don't belong to discussions of culture. . . . The Ellington sidemen mention a number of white jazzmen who influenced their styles. It was the music, the style, the ability to execute that was important. If a white musician sounded good; if he had the facility with his instrument, you took what you could use — just as they took what they could use from us. Jazz is Afro-American in origin, but it's more American than some folks want to admit." [25]

Recall, for instance, Ellison's discussion of Charlie Christian's rise to national prominence. Christian, who learned how to play guitar in Oklahoma City, would have remained a local celebrity, Ellison suggests, if he had not met Benny Goodman. According to the jazz historian Ted Gioia, Goodman first saw Christian as "an impossible rube," but when Christian began to play, Goodman, a perceptive musician and imaginative entrepreneur, heard his originality and signed him up. [26]

As Goodman got to know Christian, he must have seen reflections of his own life in Christian's. Like Christian, Goodman had begun playing as a member of his family's band. Both musicians grew up poor. Chicago was a city of immigrants. Benny Goodman was the ninth of twelve children. His family lived in an impoverished section known for its ethnic gangs. [27]

Gioia concludes that music was Goodman's way out of the ghetto, and in crucial aspects despite substantial differences, Goodman's and Christian's lives mirror each other in ways that Ellison's and Christian's do not. The similarities between Goodman's and Christian's large and impoverished musical families and the bleakness of their respective communities seem like inventions of Ellison's imagination. The Christian-Goodman connection is exemplary of Ellison's characterization of American culture as a series of "deceptive metamorphoses and blending of identities, values, life styles." [28] By 1939, when Christian joined Goodman's sextet, the Swing Era, for which Goodman receives considerable (and justifiable) credit as the "King of Swing," was rapidly accelerating. However, Goodman's pivotal role has been both praised and damned. He had previously hired

Fletcher Henderson, a talented black arranger and bandleader whose band had recently folded. Hiring Henderson was an inspired artistic and entrepreneurial choice, as well as a social gamble. He thereby integrated his white band while running the risk of driving away prejudiced white fans.

On the other hand, Goodman has been accused of stealing and exploiting black talent. Fletcher Henderson, for example, was a gifted arranger of rhythmic jazz for his dance orchestra. His band frequently played in ballrooms and dance halls like New York's Roseland. Henderson's musical intelligence and range had been enhanced by some of the most talented black jazzmen of his day. As Gioia notes: "Henderson's reed section featured, for greater or lesser stints, Coleman Hawkins, Lester Young, Ben Webster, Chu Berry and Benny Carter — one could make a case for their being the five greatest saxophonists of their day. His brass players during these years included Louis Armstrong, Roy Eldridge, Henry 'Red' Allen, Rex Stewart, Tommy Ladnier, Dickie Wells, J. C. Higginbothan, Joe Smith, Benny Morton, and Jimmy Harrison."[29] Henderson brought his extraordinary knowledge of jazz and dance music across the racial barrier into Goodman's sextet. It would have been impossible, under racial circumstances, for Henderson to succeed with his own band as quickly as Goodman did.[30] Yet it is also unlikely that Goodman would have succeeded without the rhythmic innovations created for dance halls and mastered by black musicians like Henderson and Armstrong.

The Christian-Goodman connection leads us to other Ellisonian paradoxes. We have noted how, while learning to play the guitar in Oklahoma City, Christian was deeply influenced by Lester Young's breathtaking performances. Benny Green writes that Young gives considerable credit to Frank Trumbauer and Bud Freeman, two white musicians who influenced his playing. Green concludes: "It seems that in Lester the process became apparent for the first time of the customary racial handing down of jazz being reversed. Lester represented a generation of urbanized Negroes whose attitude to life as well as jazz was profoundly different from men who had travelled afield with the music of New Orleans. In Lester the racial lines of jazz style began to get blurred over."[31]

Deeply influenced by the improvisational solos of black jazz players, Benny Goodman also aided and abetted the blurring of the lines by seizing a golden American opportunity. If swing music, with its rhythmic dance beats, was partly created by the innovations of Louis Armstrong and Fletcher Henderson, Benny Goodman became the "King of Swing" because he saw that a revolution was under way in American popular culture and took advantage of it. John Hasse explains what happened: "Tapping into a pent-up demand for genuinely rhythmic music, Goodman helped ignite a national craze for swing. Swing became a way of life for countless young people who sought out radio broadcasts from remote locations, followed their favorite bands, auditioned the latest records . . . trekked off to famed dance halls, . . . and generally reveled in the music." Dancing became a part of American courtship rituals, "the number of jukeboxes in the United States jumped from 25,000 in 1933 to 300,000 in 1939, by then consuming 13 million discs a year. . . . From a low of 6 million discs sold in 1933, sales surged to 33 million in 1938, and 127 million in 1941." [32] These dramatic increases suggest that something major was happening in American culture. The years partly overlap the period — 1939 to 1942 — that Charlie Christian spent with the Benny Goodman Sextet.

From the Ellisonian perspective, the rhythmic patterns of virtuosity of influential players like Henderson, Armstrong, Christian, and Goodman; the glamorous invention and popularity of the jukebox; the ready access of millions of Americans to thirty-five-cent disks — together tell a complex and exemplary American story of cultural exchange, a story illustrative of the central themes recurring in Ellison's essays, fiction, and interviews. In 1976, Ellison was asked when he had realized that blues and jazz had "an effect on the image that Americans had of themselves." He responds by telling the story of Louis Armstrong coming to Oklahoma City in 1929. Ellison was a teenager and says: "The bandstand in our segregated dance hall was suddenly full of white women. They were wild for his music and nothing like that had ever happened in our town before. His music was our music but they saw it as theirs too, and were willing to break the law to get to it. So you can see that Armstrong's music was affecting attitudes and values that had no immediate relationship to it." [33]

The teenagers, white or black, in Ellison's Oklahoma world of 1929 may not have recognized (in technical musical terms) that they were hearing something different, something more, in Armstrong's mastery of rhythmic phrasing or even his scat singing. But around 1929, Armstrong had begun performing and recording such songs as

"I Can't Give You Anything but Love," "Ain't Misbehavin'," "Sweet-hearts on Parade," and "Between the Devil and the Deep Blue Sea."[34] Armstrong and Duke Ellington are jazz giants who loom large in Elli-son's creative imagination and his overall sense of American culture. He rightly views them as artists dedicated to the highest standards of musicianship. But he also sees them as original American personali-ties who achieved cultural status beyond Christian, Young, and even Goodman. They were highly influential individuals upon whom American history conspired to act itself out, shaping them as they— with trumpet, piano, body and soul—definitively shaped it.

Jazz Icons
Ellison on Duke Ellington, Louis Armstrong, and Charlie Parker

Duke Ellington wrote music . . . in all 12 known keys and some keys that are still unknown; wrote music about romantic nights under Paris skies; . . . wrote music to accompany movies, television shows, ballets, broadway shows, and the exercise of horizontal options; wrote music to be played in gymnasiums, street parades, charades, wrote sacred music about the human experience; if it was experienced, he stylized it; in other words, Duke Ellington had a lot on his mind.
—Wynton Marsalis, in Beyond Category: The Life and Genius of
Duke Ellington, by John Hasse

He manifested the rhythmic gait known as "swing," transformed a polyphonic folk music into a soloist art, established the expressive profundity of blues tonality, demonstrated the durable power of melodic, harmonic improvisation, and infused it with irreverent wit — for to enter the world of Louis Armstrong is, as Constance Rourke wrote of Whitman, "to touch the spirit of American popular comedy."
— Gary Giddins, Visions of Jazz: The First Century

American Masters:
Duke Ellington and Louis Armstrong

Louis Armstrong and Duke Ellington played special roles in Ellison's development. In "Homage To Duke Ellington," an occasional piece for the *Sunday Star* to honor Duke Ellington on his seventieth birthday, Ellison writes: "I remember Ellington from my high school days in Oklahoma City, first as a strangely familiar timbre of orchestral sounds issuing from phonograph records and radio. Familiar because beneath the stylized jungle sounds . . . there sounded the blues, and strange because the mutes, toilet plungers, and derby hats with which I was acquainted as a musician had been given a stylized elegance and extension of effect unheard of even in the music of Louis Armstrong." Ellison was studying classical music at the time — "harmony and forms of symphonic music" — and concluded: "And while we affirmed the voice of jazz and the blues despite all criticism from our teachers because they spoke to a large extent of what we felt of the life we lived most intimately, it was not until the discovery of Ellington that we had any hint that jazz possessed possibilities of a range of expressiveness comparable to that of classical European music."[1] Ellison recalls his boyhood encounter with the Duke: "Then Ellington and his great orchestra came to town — came with their uniforms, their sophistication, their skills, their golden horns; . . . came with Ivy Anderson and Ethel Waters singing and dazzling the eye with their high-brown beauty and with the richness and the bright feminine flair of their costumes and promising manners. They were news from the great wide world, an example and a goal."[2]

In his homage to Duke Ellington, Ellison harshly criticizes the Pulitzer Prize Committee's advisory board, who, in 1965, rejected a recommendation to give Ellington a special award for his forty years of contributions to American music. In American cultural history, Ellington holds an exalted place. The historian E. A. Hobsbawn writes, "Nobody but the Duke (in a peculiarly anarchically controlled symbiosis with his musicians) has produced music which is both created by the players and fully shaped by the composer. He has been so unique and so far ahead of his time that even jazz musicians sometimes fail to appreciate his originality, surprised to find some revolutionary device of modern jazz anticipated in the early 1930s."[3] Hobsbawn's assessment of Ellington's talent and influence is right on target. But his assessment benignly ignores the influence of Louis Armstrong on the development of jazz in general and Ellington's orchestra in particular.

Both musical geniuses, Ellington and Armstrong were from wholly different backgrounds. Ellington was born in Washington, D.C., in 1899. His mother, Daisy Kennedy, was herself a native of Washington, and, unlike Ellington's father, a high-school graduate. His father, James Edward Ellington, a native of North Carolina, was resourceful and hardworking. He held a series of jobs and, Ellison has noted, sometimes served as a butler at the White House.[4] Ellington led a comfortable middle-class life. In his biography of Ellington, John Hasse reports: "According to Rex Stewart, who later played cornet with the Duke Ellington orchestra, people who lived in Northwest [Ellington's Washington neighborhood] were the lighter-complexioned people with better-type jobs, such as school teachers, postmen, clerks or in government service."[5] Ellington studied music and painting as a teenager. Indeed he at first wanted to be a painter and won a scholarship to study art at Pratt Institute.[6]

Since Ellison had originally enrolled in Tuskegee to study symphonic composition with William Dawson, Ellington, as composer and orchestra leader, was deeply inspiring. In "Homage to Duke Ellington," Ellison calls attention to his boyhood memory of the "uniforms and golden horns" of the Duke's orchestra but also points out the "sophistication" of the Duke's artistry. He calls it "news from the great wide world." This "news" inspired Ellison, his boyhood friend Charlie Christian, and African Americans throughout the United States. Ellison writes: "I wish that those who write so knowledgeably about Negro boys having no masculine figures with whom to identify would consider the long national and international career of Ellington and his band, and the thousands of one-night stands played in the black communities in this nation. Where in the white community, in *any* white community, could there have been found examples such as these? Who were so worldly, who so elegant, who so mockingly creative? Who were so skilled at their trade and who treated social limitations in their paths with greater disdain."[7]

Ellington, an ambassador of music with a common touch, spread culture as he went. He became a splendid model, a grand American mentor. Small wonder that Ellison's meeting with Duke Ellington intensified his yearning to attend college in order to become a composer of symphonies. After Ellison enrolled at Tuskegee Institute, Ellington and his orchestra came to the segregated Alabama campus: "I shook his hand and talked briefly with him of my studies and my dreams . . . those of us who talked with him were renewed in our determination to make our names in music."[8]

When Ellison refers to Ellington and his orchestra as cultural ambassadors and worldly, elegant, and creative role models for "Negro boys," he interprets Ellington's orchestra as a cultural phenomenon more profound than the marvelous music they played. The orchestra was a uniquely American invention beyond its glorious sound, at once defined and dependent upon music, and a transformative cultural force beyond lush melodies. In its transcendent excellence, it challenged racial boundaries. Much of this can be explained by the quality of the orchestra's music. But the orchestra's manner of dress, the arrangement of the musicians on stage, and the stage personas of various ensembles and soloists were as critical to the success of Ellington's live performances as the blending of the musicians' "tonal personalities."[9] Ellington was not only an accomplished musician but also a successful entertainer and a clever entrepreneur. He took as much care arranging his orchestra on stage as he did the musical score. The music and the collective image were one in a live performance — each critical to overall success.

In *Swing Out: Great Negro Dance Bands*, Gene Fernett describes the cultural significance of orchestras like Ellington's: "Prior to 1934, if there were any hope at all for better things in American dance music, it was held by the Negro bands of the time, principally those of Duke Ellington, Fletcher Henderson, Jimmie Lunceford and a handful of others. Whether the band was spawned in Washington, D.C., as was Ellington's; New York, as were Henderson's and Webb's; or came roaring in from the Midwest, as did Basie, Kirk, and McKinney's Cotton Pickers, the band had two things in common. . . . It was a Negro outfit, and it was a magnificent orchestra."[10]

The distinctive character of Ellington's orchestra meant something more than looking good on stage. The cultural power of his orchestra was rooted in his performers' maintaining a fidelity to musical excellence and their unique stage presentations. Ivy Anderson, a singer who joined the Ellington orchestra for a four-week tour in 1931 and stayed for twelve years, spoke of Ellington's influence on her style and character: "When I first started with Ellington . . . I used to wear colored dresses. When he suggested I wear only white, I tried it out and found it so effective that I've been doing it ever since. . . . Duke helped me tremendously in molding my style of singing. When I joined his band, I was just an ordinary singer of popular songs. Duke suggested that I find a character and maintain it. . . . The combination of these two things resulted in the type of songs I'm still doing today. The first one I sang that way was 'Minnie the Moocher,' when the boys in the band worked out the idea of talking back to me while I was singing. . . . And I'll never forget the first record I made — 'It Don't Mean a Thing If It Ain't Got That Swing.' "[11]

When Anderson refers to "finding a character," she brings to mind Ellison's characterization of the jazz musician's "true academy," the "apprenticeship" and the series of "ordeals" and "initiation ceremonies" the musician necessarily faces acquiring technique and thereby finding her "self-determined identity." Anderson's replacing her colorful dresses with the white dresses that became part of her onstage presence and the adjustments she made in her singing technique to achieve and maintain character exemplify Ellison's sense of the jazz musician's apprenticeship. But Anderson's comments also provide evidence of improvisation at work. Her version of "Minnie the Moocher" became more dramatic and alluring when the sidemen in the band started "talking back" to her while she was singing. Their back talk has long since become a standard feature of the song.

Another member of Ellington's orchestra, Joseph "Tricky Sam" Nanton, also alludes to "character," the continual projection of a consistent tonal personality and stage persona. "Tricky Sam" Nanton is known for perfecting the growl style of trombone playing, the use of a plunger-style mute to duplicate and mock the sounds of the human voice. Nanton was schooled in the style by Ellington's early trumpet player, Bubber Miley. After Miley's death, Nanton taught the growl style to trumpeter Cootie Williams, and it thereby became one of the characteristic features of Ellington's brass sound. Nanton says: "Around 1921 I heard Johnny Dunn playing a trumpet with a plunger, so I decided the plunger should be good on trombone. . . . I got the plunger all right, but it sounded so terrible everybody howled. . . . After a couple of months they began to see the light when I finally came up with something in tune. . . . Today trombonists try the plunger and discover it's way out of tune. . . . They have to violate all the principles of trombone playing to use the plunger properly. . . . You have to play about a quarter-tune flatter. . . . You have to use the lip too, and work it out until the desired effect is obtained." Nanton's description of learning the growl style demonstrates the power of improvisation and the necessity of stern discipline in the face of technical obstacles. He says: "It is not advisable to use a plunger and be a good trombone player unless the musician is going to use that style exclusively." He emphasizes as well the learning of technique via apprenticeship —

the growl style moving from one musician to the next and from one instrument to another. We see a trajectory and tradition involving Miley and Dunn, then Nanton, on to Cootie Williams — from trumpeters to trombonist and back to a trumpeter.[12]

In his homage to Ellington, Ellison remains true to his role as custodian of culture. Performers like Ivie Anderson and Nanton were necessary for the invention of Ellington's music and the presentation of his colorful show. Ellison refers to the bright trail of magic Ellington brought and left behind when he "played thousands of one-night stands in the black communities." Ellison had three inspiring encounters with the Duke before becoming a successful writer: He saw Ellington's great orchestra during his boyhood in Oklahoma City; he chatted with him while he was a music student at Tuskegee Institute in Alabama; and he visited Ellington at the beginning of his stay in New York City in 1933. To him, Duke Ellington is "a culture hero, a musical magician, who worked his powers through his mastery of form, nuance and style, a charismatic figure whose personality influenced even those who had no immediate concern with the art of jazz."[13]

Long before the Pulitzer Prize committee's advisory board rejected a recommendation that Duke Ellington be given an award, Ellington had achieved, by Ellison's standards, profound cultural authority. Ellison had long before drawn his own conclusions about the true value of Ellington's music and the scope of his influence. He had also noted the Duke's charisma and generosity. In the Ellington homage Ellison writes of his encounter (in 1933) with Ellington shortly after his arrival in New York: "Later I met Langston Hughes, who took me up to Sugar Hill to visit the Duke in his apartment. Much to my delight, the great musician remembered me, was still apologetic because of the lateness of the band's arrival at Tuskegee and asked me what he could do to aid the music department. I said that we were sadly deficient in our library of classical scores and recordings, and he offered to make the school a gift of as extensive a library of recordings as was needed."[14]

The awe Ellison felt facing the "great musician" was inspired by the unexpected intimacy of the moment. He was charmed by the Duke's memory and his generosity. Ellington was also probably impressed by a young black man yearning to compose symphonies. He could see too that he had played a role in fueling the flames of Ellison's musical ambition. This image, the crisscrossing of their artistic paths, highlights again Ellison's belief in American possibility.

Like the Pulitzer Prize committee, the Tuskegee Music Department failed to understand or recognize the nature of Ellington's talent and his remarkable contribution to American culture. Ellison criticizes the Tuskegee Music Department for refusing to pursue Ellington's gift of scores and recordings: "It was an offer which I passed on to Tuskegee with great enthusiasm, but which, for some reason, perhaps because it had not come directly from Ellington himself, or perhaps because several people in the department regarded jazz as an inferior form of music, was rejected. That his was a genuine gesture I had no doubt." [15] Near the end of his homage, Ellison returns to the Pulitzer committee's neglect: "When the Pulitzer Prize committee refused to give him a special award for music (a decision which led certain members of that committee to resign), Ellington remarked, 'Fate is being kind to me. Fate doesn't want me to be too famous too young,' a quip as mocking of our double standards, hypocrisies, and pretensions as the dancing of those slaves who, looking through the windows of a plantation manor house from the yard, imitated the steps so gravely performed by the masters within and then added to them their own special flair, burlesquing the white folks and then going on to force the steps into a choreography uniquely their own." [16]

The allusion to southern mansions and manners produced by slavery connects the genesis of jazz, no less than its reception or recognition, to Ellison's overall theme of the influence of blacks in American culture. His theme of invisibility also surfaces here. The Ellington of "East Saint Louis Toodle-oo," "Solitude," and "Sophisticated Lady" remains outside or beyond academic and cultural institutional approval. Like the slaves creating new dance steps, Ellington and his music symbolize this ongoing cultural paradox: "The whites, looking out at the activity in the yard, thought that they were being flattered by imitation and were amused by the incongruity of tattered blacks dancing courtly steps, while missing completely the fact that before their eyes a European cultural form was becoming Americanized, undergoing a metamorphosis through the mocking activity of a people partially sprung from Africa. So, blissfully unaware, the whites laughed while the blacks danced out their mocking reply." [17]

By returning to such defining circumstances in the nation's past, Ellison focuses on the hierarchical relationship and the ambiguous nature of the dynamic between blacks and whites in the United States. It is a miniature of the vast American canvas, a large and crowded picture evoking the bewildering fate of African Americans and thereby depicting the history and potential future of America with its "double standards, hypocrisies and pretensions."

The miniature is characteristic of Ellison's panoramic view. The two groups, black slaves and white masters, are pictured together. The whites, seemingly in total control, are "inside" dancing, enjoying the leisure made possible by the free labor of anonymous slaves. The black slaves are ostensibly "outside" looking in — locked, by law and custom, out of the social compact, denied the full promise of American democracy. The slaves nonetheless watch, improvise, and create new steps of their own. While their masters play, the slaves find, in Ellison's words, a certain "freedom within restrictions." He dramatizes the way in which culture, like the humans who invent it, always escapes across the artificial boundaries prescribed by law and by custom.

American culture is an ongoing narrative of such unexpected creations and variations. Ellison believes that the nature of American genius can only be accurately understood if one looks beyond the expected norms and the usual places. In his view, the Pulitzer committee's advisory board simply failed to perceive the power and creativity of jazz, the country's most significant indigenous art form. Ironically, the committee's members were already the beneficiaries of Ellington's music, whether or not they knew or acknowledged it. Songs such as "East Saint Louis Toodle-oo," "Sophisticated Lady," and "In a Sentimental Mood," among others, had become American standards.

Long before the 1965 Pulitzer Prize rejection, Ellington had achieved, by Ellison's standards, profound cultural validity, confirmed symbolically by his orchestra's first big tour of the South in 1933. Starting in Dallas, the tour demonstrated precisely what Ellison means when he refers to the ironies and contradictions, "the deceptive metamorphoses" seen in American culture. Ellington came South after a tour of smashing success in London and on Broadway. For Ellison, the arrival of the orchestra in Dallas, via London and New York, highlights two of his major themes — possibility and ambiguity.

Ellington's tour of the South was promoted by his New York agent, Irving Mills. John Hasse says that Mills "made sure the newspapers on the band's itinerary were well supported with advance publicity." [18] The press releases stressed not only certain musical characteristics, but biographical details, humorous and laudatory, of all band members. They revealed that several band members were college graduates and that others had attended conservatories: "Freddy Jenkins . . . nicknamed 'Posey" because of his posing ways . . . maladjusted New Jersey real estate agent, another Wilberforce graduate, always writing letters in the world's fanciest hand." [19]

Hasse describes the tour's beginning at Dallas's Majestic Theatre on September 3, 1933. In one week, the Majestic broke its previous record of ticket sales, grossing twenty-two thousand dollars: "The *Dallas News* reviewer was enthralled, calling Ellington 'something of an African Stravinsky' and asserting that five Ellington compositions — *Ring Dem Bells, Sophisticated Lady, It Don't Mean a Thing, Black and Tan Fantasy* and *Mood* — 'erased the color line' between jazz and classical music." The reporter adds: "Segregation ruled at Ellington's performances. At Dallas's Ice Palace, one dance was held for whites and a few days later another was held for African-Americans, at which white 'spectators' were allowed to sit in a reserved area. There was a special midnight show at the Majestic . . . with a 200-voice black choir whose program included several Negro spirituals; the balcony was reserved for blacks." [20]

This ambiguous American scene of black talent temporarily breaking down racial barriers recalls Ellison's boyhood memory of Armstrong's playing in Oklahoma City to an unexpectedly integrated audience. A paradoxical yet definitive American moment, it is duplicated with added dimensions in the southern tour of Ellington's orchestra. Blacks and whites briefly came together to hear the same talented black musicians, and yet social hierarchy and racial dividing lines were maintained in both Oklahoma and Texas. Black clients were allowed to pay a fee to sit in the balcony to witness a performance primarily put on for whites by Ellington's orchestra and a black choir. And white "spectators" were allowed to attend a dance held primarily for African Americans. Had an interracial couple been moved to dance publicly, a race riot would have broken out.

Ellington's orchestra is the same one that the boy Ralph Ellison saw several weeks later in Oklahoma City. The musicians — with their diverse backgrounds, college education, and varied interests beyond music — were like Americans in general, a hodgepodge of talents, complexions, weaknesses and strengths. Yet Ellison reminds us that few other bands, whether in New York or in London, let alone Texas, could create such music. But despite their talent and attraction as a principal cultural event, the musicians were essentially on their own once the show was over. They were forbidden to stay at local hotels or dine at restaurants.

Although Ellison is keenly aware of the continuing existence of segregation and potential threats of violence against black band members, he does not emphasize it. However, some critics do. Shane White and Graham White describe a violent attack: "Ellington and his orchestra made a lasting impression on a young Ralph Ellison in Oklahoma City. . . . But not everyone in the South appreciated this 'news' as much as Ellison did. The *Chicago Defender* reported in 1922 that members of a black band had been beaten up outside a Miami hotel. . . . Their white assailants had warned them: 'We'll teach you niggers to come here dressed in your white flannels and tweed coats, playing for our dances and looking at our pretty white women. Now, go back up North and tell all your nigger friends." [21] As late as 1960, while passing through Connecticut, Armstrong was denied access to a bathroom by the owner of a restaurant. Herb Snitzer, who went along on the tour as a photographer said afterward, "I will never forget the look on Louis's face. Hero that he was, world-famous, a favorite to millions of people, America's single most identifiable entertainer, and yet excluded in the most humiliating fashion from a common convenience." [22]

Ellison stresses how black jazz musicians, like African Americans in general, used their discipline and imagination to persevere and triumph. Despite segregation and the ongoing threat of violence, some black musicians remained undaunted and in imaginative ways turned the system on its head. Gene Fernett quotes Billy Butler, a light-skinned Negro, who traveled with a group of five members of a vaudeville troupe called the Sheiks of Araby. Forbidden to stay in decent hotels, they had to stay overnight at rooming houses that, according to Butler, "were literally crawling with vermin." Fernett describes how Butler ingeniously solved their problem. In Ohio one day after the Sheiks had finished their performance, Butler instructed them to keep their Arab costumes on and follow him:

Butler walked his incredulous band of followers to the finest cafe he could find. . . . "In here," Butler said, waving his sheiks through the door, and "Act like you don't speak English."

There was a hushed, reverential silence in the restaurant as the dark-skinned guests seated themselves. Had they been dressed as mere American Negroes, they would have been ejected. But now they were exotic; they were Far Easterners, and very acceptable to the management.

"Them no speak English . . . Me order for all," Butler reassured the bowing waiter.

Thereafter Butler and his fellow Sheiks of Araby used the ruse to eat at fine restaurants and stay at good hotels on many other occasions. Butler says: "We kept those outfits well laundered from then on . . . and had plenty of changes of garb, because those things were doing double duty: On stage for a two-a-day vaudeville; as our ticket to hotels and restaurants after the shows." [23]

The preceding account is both symbolic and worthy of Ellison's inventive imagination. Yet the actual event and others like it, involve brutal facts of American history. Armstrong and Ellington surely developed the discipline and guile to escape and, sometimes necessarily, to bear the full burden of, such racial discrimination. Ellington's career, which lasted for so long and went through so many trying and glorious phases, was in itself a grand American story of discipline, human insight, and survival.

Mocking Entertainers:
Ellison on Louis Armstrong
and Charlie Parker

Like Ellington, Armstrong and Charlie Parker lived and died for jazz. Both geniuses, they created technical and stylistic innovations that were deeply influential among jazz artists. In *Visions of Jazz*, Gary Giddins succinctly captures Armstrong's lowly beginnings: "Armstrong was born in the poorest section of New Orleans, on a dark block of wooden ramshackle houses called Jane Alley, between Perdido and Gravier Streets, on August 4, 1901. His father left him at once; his mother went to work in a nearby red-light district, leaving him in the care of his paternal grandmother until he was old enough to go to school, at which time he moved in with his mother, his younger sister and a round of 'stepfathers.'" [24]

Armstrong worked a number of odd jobs, earning enough money to buy his first cornet at age eleven. He fell in love with the sound of various street bands and was deeply attracted to the band and trumpet playing of King Oliver. By the time Armstrong was sixteen, and with the tutelage of King Oliver and another trumpeter, Kid Ory, "he was beginning to master the instrument." [25] His mastery of the cornet and trumpet and his presence as a soloist changed jazz music forever. Numerous jazz critics have noted how Armstrong created the paradigm of the solo as an integral part in jazz performance. Less has been said about how his style and technical innovations influenced orchestral arrangements and musicians other than trumpet players. These aspects of his talent, let alone the quality of his singing, had a direct impact on Ellington's developing sense of composing and arrangement, his search for a sound that would always swing.

Writing of Armstrong's work with Fletcher Henderson's band during the 1920s, Ted Gioia concludes: "Brass players were the first to feel the heat of Armstrong's rising star; but, as with Charlie Parker's innovation twenty years later, Armstrong's contributions eventually spread to every instrument in the band. Don Redman's arrangements, Coleman Hawkins' saxophone work — one by one, the converts were won. Armstrong the sideman? Not really. Armstrong was a leader . . . during his time with the Henderson band." [26] Furthermore Laurence Bergreen reports that once Armstrong's reputation grew, Ellington "repeatedly brought his orchestra down to the Roseland to hear Louis blow." [27] Ellington said, "When Smack's [Fletcher Henderson's] band hit town, the guys had never heard anything just like it." [28] Unlike Ellington, however, Armstrong lacked the administrative skill and personality to become a great band leader.

For Ellison, Armstrong and Parker, or "Satchmo" and "Bird," represent in turn the positive and negative or the marvelous and terrible dimensions of jazz life. Even allowing for his predicaments and defeats, Armstrong's was a long triumphant life and career. Parker's, in contrast, was a bright blue flame, a brief and widely publicized spectacle of musical extravagance and self-destruction. Ironically, Parker's fatal flaw was inexorably tied to his relentless attempt to escape the tradition of American minstrelsy which, he believed, Armstrong's performances vividly personified. Parker, along with Miles Davis and other younger musicians, responded negatively to the older generation of jazzmen. "They were intensely concerned that their identity as Negroes placed no restrictions upon the music they played or the manner in which they used their talent," Ellison writes. "They were concerned, they said, with art, not entertainment. Especially were they resentful of Louis Armstrong, whom (confusing the spirit of his music with his clowning) they considered an Uncle Tom." [29]

Ellison does not share their view of Armstrong's "clowning." He believes that Armstrong understood and thereby maintained a private and ironic distance from the smiling and outrageously costumed persona he often projected. The stark contrast between the entertainer and the private man, or between the clown and the true artist, was invariably expressed through his dazzling and dignified music. "Armstrong's clownish license and intoxicating powers," Ellison writes, "are almost Elizabethan; he takes liberties with kings, queens and presidents; emphasizes the physicality of his music with sweat, spittle and facial contortions; he performs the magical feat of making romantic melody issue from a throat of gravel; and some few years ago was recommending to all and sundry his personal physic, 'Pluto Water,' as a purging way to health, happiness and international peace." [30]

Ellison uses Armstrong's life and music in "On Bird, Bird-Watching, and Jazz" to strike a revelatory contrast to the portrait he paints of Charlie Parker. Published in 1962, Ellison's essay, a review of the testimonial anthology *Bird: The Legend of Charlie Parker* (1962), gives the saxophonist his artistic due. Ellison says that Parker, "as an improvisor," had "as marked an influence on jazz as Louis Armstrong, Coleman Hawkins or Johnny Hodges." Comparing Parker to a mockingbird, he writes: "His playing was characterized by velocity, by long-continued successions of notes and phrases, by swoops, bleats, echoes, rapidly repeated bebops — I mean rebopped bebops — by mocking mimicry of other jazzmen's styles, and by interpolations of motifs from extraneous melodies, all of which added up to a dazzling display of wit, satire, burlesque and pathos. Further, he was as expert at issuing his improvisations from the dense brush as from the extreme treetops of the harmonic landscape, and there was, without doubt, as irrepressible a mockery in his personal conduct as in his music." [31]

The similarity between Armstrong and Parker, with one exception, stops at the power and influential nature of their musical genius. It has been widely corroborated that Armstrong was a habitual smoker of marijuana. He believed in its medicinal and music-inducing powers. Parker seemed, if not consciously devoted, equally addicted to heroin. So Armstrong, the clownish exponent of "health, happiness, and international peace," oddly begets Parker, who responds in self-destructive reaction. Ellison calls Parker "a most ingratiating and difficult man": "According to his witnesses, he stretched the limits of human contradiction beyond belief. He was lovable and hateful, considerate and callous; he stole from friends and benefactors and borrowed without conscience, often without repaying, and yet was generous to absurdity. He could be most kind to younger musicians or utterly crushing in his contempt for their ineptitude. He was passive and yet quick to pull a knife and pick a fight." [32]

Apart from the extreme contrasts in their respective personalities, Armstrong and Parker had wholly different approaches to their audiences. Ellison's primary concern is to show how Parker and other younger jazzmen were "confused," unable to see the complexity of Armstrong's persona — how the smiling trumpeter was at once a clowning entertainer and a consummate artist. For even as he played the role of various clowns — whether performing in leopard skin and plume in the movie *Rhapsody in Black and Blue* (1932) or as a horse groom in *Goin' Places* (1938) or bewigged and white-faced as the King of the Zulus in the Mardi Gras parade — the lyrical sound of his music possessed a life and definitive American authority of its own. Ellison concludes: "But when they fastened the epithet Uncle Tom upon Armstrong's music they confused artistic quality with questions of personal conduct, a confusion which would ultimately reduce their own music to the mere matter of race. By rejecting Armstrong they thought to rid themselves of the entertainer's role. And by way of getting rid of the role they demanded, in the name of their racial identity, a purity of status which by definition is impossible for the performing artist." He notes further that the younger musicians' confusion about Armstrong led to "a grim comedy of racial manners, with the musicians employing a calculated surliness and rudeness," and that white audiences soon viewed the rudeness as part of their entertaining routine. [33]

To Ellison, Parker was the prince par excellence of the new generation: "No jazzman, not even Miles Davis, struggled harder to escape the entertainer's role than Charlie Parker." Ellison sees in Parker's relationship to his youthful white audience an "ironic reversal." All appearances to the contrary, Parker became, if not an Uncle Tom, a "sacrificial figure" with a cult following. Ellison views Parker as a "white hero" because he embodied the disaffections of white middle-class "jazzniks." Louis Armstrong perfected the gliss and practiced hitting high C's and G's to avoid disappointing those who came to see and hear "the World's Greatest Trumpet Player." Parker's fans came to hear the fantastic new music he played, but they also came to witness "the world's greatest junky" and the "supreme hipster." [34] To his cult, Ellison says, Bird was "a suffering, psychically wounded, law-breaking, life-affirming hero," an alienated and "obsessed outsider" — a Negro, addict, and innovative jazz artist. He believes that Bird "invokes a sense of tragic fellowship in those who saw in his agony a ritualization of their own fears, rebellions and hunger for creativity." [35]

To Ellison, Charlie Parker emerges as a modern descendant of Uncle Tom. He is Uncle Tom reincarnated in hot flesh and jazzy spirit, an embodiment through ritualization of both the virtues and the vices of his white audience. Ellison sees a pattern of self-destruction in Parker's "struggles to escape" Armstrong's "make-believe role of clown." Bird lives on as "a sacrificial figure whose struggles against personal chaos, on stage and off, served as entertainment for a ravenous, sensation-starved, culturally disoriented public which had but the slightest notion of its real significance." Ellison gives us a sense of the high price Parker paid when he writes, "While he slowly died (like a man dismembering himself with a dull razor on a spotlighted stage) from the ceaseless conflict from which issued both his art and his destruction, his public reacted as though he were doing much the same thing as those saxophonists who hoot and honk and roll on the floor. In the end he had no private life and his most magic moments were drained of human significance." [36]

Ellison's critique is dispassionate. But he is hardly attempting to clean up the general image of the jazz world. In "The Golden Age, Time Past," he explains that the lives of many famous jazzmen were too sensational for respectability. He recalls how Charlie Parker "coughed up his life and died — as incredibly as the leopard which Hemingway tells us was found 'dried and frozen' near the summit of Mount Kilimanjaro." [37] Still, despite their stormy lives, or partly because of them, the musicians created music that will supersede their legends. Much of this happened at various jazz clubs. Ellison refers to the jam sessions routinely welcomed and encouraged at Minton's, where Parker often played, as "the jazzman's true academy": "Here it is more meaningful to speak not of courses of study, of grades and degrees, but of apprenticeship, ordeals, initiation ceremonies, of rebirth."[38] Perhaps Ellison should also have pointed out the connection between Parker and Lester Young. While an apprentice, and before his arrival in New York, Parker learned — note by note — Lester Young's recorded solos.[39]

But as Ellison sees it, even Young, the great and influential Prez, does not rival Armstrong and Ellington. Through their sustained virtuosity, they became cultural icons in the United States and abroad. In their written correspondence, Ellison and Albert Murray, the writer's friend and fellow jazz fan, frequently discussed various jazz recordings and concerts. They made suggestions to and complimented each other about their writing on jazz and the blues. And in letter after letter, they celebrated the remarkable achievements of Ellington and Armstrong. On June 2, 1957, Ellison, then a fellow at the American Academy in Rome, wrote Murray a long letter. The letter is genuinely Ellisonian in its range of topics — a reference to Faulkner's recently published novel, The Town; a mention of Steegmuller's translation of Madame Bovary; and comments on Dizzy Gillespie, Thelonious Monk, and Sugar Ray Leonard. He does not hold back on his critical evaluations of either friends or foes. After thanking Murray for sending him several jazz tapes, Ellison says: "With both Duke and Basie I could hope for better word from home." However, he later remarks: "As for the bit from Drum, I like, but suspect that here again Duke fails to make the transition from the refinement of his music over to drama — or even over to words; so that what in music would be vital ideas comes over with a slickness and hipster elegance that makes you want to go and tell the man how really good he is. . . . He should leave that element to Billy Strayhorn."[40]

Louis Armstrong comes up when Ellison tells Murray about an argument with his (Ellison's) friend Stanley Hyman, who had sent him a lecture on "Negro writing" and the folk tradition. He calls it "a very disappointing piece" and tells Murray that Hyman fails to grasp the true "work of metaphor." Ellison concludes: "He can't really see that Bessie Smith singing a good blues may deal with experience as profoundly as Eliot, with the eloquence of Eliotic poetry being expressed in her voice and phrasing. Human anguish is human anguish, love,

love; the difference between Shakespeare and lesser artists is elo-quence. . . . Which reminds me that here, way late, I've discovered Louis singing Mack the Knife. Shakespeare invented Caliban or changed himself into him — Who the hell dreamed up Louie? Some of the bop boys consider him Caliban but if he is he's a mask for a lyric poet who is much greater than most writing now." [41]

Ellison closes his letter on an intimate note. "Write about those blues," Ellison says, "and love to the girls from me and Fanny." Since Murray had informed Ellison of irregular heart rhythms that had briefly left him hospitalized, Ellison adds a solicitous postscript: "Watch that heart!" [42]

Jazz Trio
Ralph Ellison,
Romare Bearden, and
Albert Murray

It is the elegance of ritual: Bearden, Ellison
and Murray cutting the jagged grains: patchwork
figures in silhouette, blue notes in calico
and quilting under glass. What did I do
to be so black and blue? Electric blue, fire
and fuchsia in the sky. Lightning, lonesome blue.
Cut out legs, fingers and bebop eyes
shape the uncreated features of face and race.
Found objects of the territory:
Mecklenberg County to Harlem and back.
Cloth and color in piano stride

What did I do? You lived, you lived.
And the jagged grains so black and blue
open like lips about to sing.

— Melvin Dixon, "Fingering the Jagged Grains,"
  from Change of Territory

Renaissance Men:
Ralph Ellison, Romare Bearden,
and Albert Murray

In 1972, in an interview with Ralph Ellison conducted by the novelist Leon Forrest in Ellison's Harlem apartment, Forrest calls attention to "many fine pieces of African sculpture and Romare Bearden paintings."[1] Several years later, when novelist Steve Cannon inquired about Bearden's influence on his work, Ellison said that he and Bearden had met during the 1930s when they were both starting out in New York City. Their mutual interests in art, literature, jazz, sculpture, and photography led to friendship. Each mirrored the other's artistic ambitions. Yet Ellison says he never consciously tried to create the verbal equivalent of Bearden's artistic style in his writing. Bearden's influence had come primarily from his exemplary dedication to his craft: "The influence of one artist upon another . . . frequently takes other forms than that of copying or trying to do what another artist or writer does in a precise manner. . . . He [Bearden] had faith in the importance of artistic creation, and I learned something about the nature of painting from listening to his discussion of craft." [2]

New York City is the place where Romare Bearden, Ralph Ellison, and, later, Albert Murray became good friends and intellectual sparring partners. Each somehow helped hone the others' artistic and intellectual gifts. They had similar interests and experience. Murray and Bearden had served in the military — Murray in the Air Force, Bearden in the Army. And Ellison has written of his duty as a Merchant Marine. They were athletes when they were young. Ellison was a running back during his high school days. And Murray — a Tuskegee Tiger! — played football during the 1930s at that black Alabama college. Murray also played basketball while at Tuskegee. Bearden was a baseball player at Boston University.

Ellison, Bearden, and Murray shared a deep appreciation for books, art, and jazz. They were, for example, deeply inspired by Duke Ellington and his music. Bearden, like Ellison, heard him as a boy in Harlem. In "Putting Something Over Something Else," his profile of Bearden, Calvin Tomkins writes: "Growing up in Harlem of the twenties, Bearden lived and breathed the music and came to know most of the great performers. Duke Ellington, Fats Waller, Billie Holiday, Louis Armstrong, and Jelly Roll Morton were his early masters (to be joined later by Duccio, Vermeer, Delacroix, and Mondrian)." [3] Tomkins also says: "Duke Ellington was a friend of the family and bought an oil from Bearden's first formal exhibition."

However, Ellington was not the immediate inspiration for Bearden's start as a painter. In 1926, after Bearden had moved to Pittsburgh to live with his grandmother, he met Eugene, a boy who had been left crippled by infantile paralysis. Eugene and Bearden became playmates, and Eugene was always around Bearden's grandmother's house. One day Eugene showed Bearden some breathtaking pictures he had drawn on sheets of brown paper: "He'd done one drawing of a house of prostitution not far from where we lived, run by a woman named Sadie. . . . Eugene had drawn Sadie's house with the façade cut off, so you could see in all the rooms. And somebody had shot off a pistol, and the bullet was going all through the house. Women were on top of men and the bullet was going through them, into the next room and the next until it came down through the ceiling into the front parlor, and Sadie had her pocketbook open, and the bullet had turned into coins and was dropping into her pocketbook." Bearden asked Eugene to teach him to draw and Eugene became his eager instructor: "My grandmother set up a table in my room, and Eugene and I would go and draw every day. All his drawings were about what happened in Sadie's house, and I was just trying religiously to copy what he did. After a week or so, my grandmother . . . took one look, and she grabbed all those drawings and threw them into the furnace. She said, 'Eugene, where did you ever see anything like that?' Eugene said, 'My mother is a whore. She works over at Sadie's place.'"[4] This colorful page from Bearden's life story has an Ellisonian ring about it. It is a true allegory of the wound and the bow vividly demonstrating the unexpected influences on artistic genius while showing the tragic and triumphant paradoxes of a crippled boy's life.

The Novelist and the Painter:
Shared Visions of Jazz and Art

Indeed a recurrent image in Bearden's work (recalling Eugene's drawings) is a picture of apartment buildings with the façades removed — revealing the private lives of the diverse dwellers within. Bearden's artistic technique — his creation and distortion of images, forms, and materials, no less than his conscious references to the great masters — surely caught Ellison's attention. Furthermore, Ellison's memory of Armstrong and Ellington in Oklahoma City and Bearden's of the same jazzmen in Harlem were sources of mutual inspiration. "I often heard sounds of a piano from an open window," Bearden says, "and in the warm weather there were likely to be two or three musicians on a street corner playing for whatever onlookers might drop in the hat." Oklahoma City was a hothouse of jazz, but so was Harlem. Bearden writes: "There were also great bands —

Fletcher Henderson, Duke Ellington, Sammy Stewart, Don Redman, Earl Hines, Louis Armstrong, all of whom played at the Lafayette Theatre on 132nd Street and Seventh Avenue, or at the Savoy Ballroom on 141st Street and Lenox Avenue. Alberta Hunter, Bessie and Clara Smith, and Ethel Waters were among the great ladies whom I heard sing the blues."[5]

Furthermore, Bearden and Ellison studied the music of the best jazz musicians. They were attuned to the musicians' creation of new musical forms, sounds, and rhythms. Their admiration went beyond a yearning to imitate or copy artistic techniques. The musicians personified standards of vocational excellence and visions of personal and artistic possibility. Thinking metaphorically about the process of jazz aided Bearden in his art, and he sometimes appropriated what jazz or individual jazz artists suggested as technical devices. Put another way, one artist — musician, writer, or painter — can perceive or imagine another's artistic ideal, seeing through or beyond execution to the moment of artistic conception. The perception in that inspired moment can then be used to carry out what Bearden calls a "transmutation" of the conceptual ideal in his own work.

Bearden once said that "abstract expressionism is very close to the aesthetics of jazz. That's the feeling you get from it — involvement, personality, improvisation, rhythm, color."[6] Similarly, in "Jazz and the New York School," Mona Hadler notes the impact of jazz on abstract expressionism. She writes: "Before Willem de Kooning left Holland for New York in 1930, he conjured up an America of 'broad clean streets in a glare of white light and everywhere the sound of Louis Armstrong's trumpet.'" Other artists — including Jimmy Ernst, Carl Holty, Franz Kline, Piet Mondrian, Larry Rivers, Seymour Lipton, Stuart Davis, and Jackson Pollock — were also deeply influenced by jazz. According to Lee Krasner, Pollock's wife, he would listen to jazz "day and night for three days running." Pollock felt that jazz was "the only other really creative thing" happening in the United States.[7]

Bearden often mentioned how his fellow artist and friend Stuart Davis helped him to appreciate and use models and techniques taken from jazz. Stuart Davis, a fan of the jazz pianist Earl Hines, suggested that Bearden study Hines's phrasing: "I showed a watercolor to Stuart Davis, and he pointed out that I had treated both the left and right sides of the painting in the same way. After that, at Davis' suggestion,

I listened for hours to recordings of Earl Hines at the piano. Finally, I was able to block out the melody and concentrate on the silences between the notes. I found that this was very helpful to me in the transmutation of sound into colors and in the placement of objects in my paintings and collages."[8]

Something happened to Bearden in listening to Hines, his blocking out the melody and hearing "the silences between notes," that inspired a technical perception of immediate artistic use. Tomkins concludes: "In Bearden's painting, the separations between colors, or between different values of a color, are expressive in this way. Like Hines, Bearden is a virtuoso of the interval."[9] Ellison, as a trained musician, no doubt experienced similar perceptions which inspired transmutations in his writing. Both the novelist and the painter searched for examples of technical virtuosity among artists who fully exploited their subjects or themes. In this sense, for Ellison and Bearden alike, jazz led to perceptions of the multifarious ways of presenting the complexity of human experience. Each consciously tried to rescue the collective image of African Americans from the narrow realm of stereotypes, clichés, and prejudice. Each artist studiously attempted to remain open to the full range of artistic advances, whatever their source, in order to create vivid and forceful stories and images. Each believed in drawing upon the techniques and traditions of the artists who preceded them. "Transmutation" implies something beyond the original idea of the other artist. It necessarily suggests technical improvisation that creates its own originality.

Ellison began as a musician and turned to writing. Bearden started out as a painter and, for a brief and confused period, attempted writing songs. Tomkins reports that during the early 1950s twenty of Bearden's songs were recorded, and his "Seabreeze" was a "substantial hit." During this period, he visited his friends Hannah Arendt and her husband, Heinrich Blucher. Blucher told Bearden: "You're wasting your life. In the first place, you don't even believe in what you're doing. Do you think Irving Berlin and Cole Porter could do what they do if they didn't believe in it?" Bearden recalled: "Hannah said I was going to wreck myself as a painter. . . . Then, one day, walking on the street, I suddenly felt I couldn't walk a step farther. The next thing I knew I was in the hospital. I asked the nurse, 'Where am I?' She said I was in the psychiatric ward at Bellevue. A doctor came by, and I asked him what had happened to me. 'You blew a fuse,' he said.

Just what Arendt and others had said was going to happen to me had happened."[10]

After his flirtation with the music business and its stressful consequences, Bearden eventually turned to making cutouts and collages. Tomkins notes: "All of Bearden's former discoveries seemed to come together in the new collage paintings: The shallow space of Byzantine mosaics, the strong forms of African sculpture, the spatial harmonies of Chinese landscapes, and most significant of all, the carefully planned structure of Vermeer and the little Dutch masters."[11] His work also owes something to that of Matisse. But some critics — reviewers and museum tourists alike — have often missed the point of Bearden's collages. The cutouts and fragments of photographs taken from magazines sometimes have been viewed simplistically as so many separate parts pasted together to form a random whole. For example, Michael Gibson, a critic for the *International Herald-Tribune*, described Bearden's collages as "peopled by black faces cut out of magazines." Bearden answers that he uses "many disparate elements" and explains the various stages involved in his work: "I build my faces, for example, from parts of African masks, animal eyes, marbles, mossy vegetation, etc. . . . I have found that when some detail, such as a hand or an eye, is taken out of its original context and is fractured and integrated into a different space and form and configuration, it acquires a plastic quality it did not have in the photograph."[12]

Bearden's artistic method goes beyond the use of found imagery. He makes the familiar strange and new through fragmentation followed by reorientation that creates integral parts of a new whole. Thus, the eye of a tiger is miraculously transformed into an eye of human perception and sensitivity. Nor does Bearden's process stop there: it is the beginning rather than the end. During his apprenticeship, he read Delacroix's journal and, like Delacroix, concluded: "I, too, could profit by systematically copying the masters of the past and of the present." Bearden preferred not to work in museums, so he "used photostats, enlarging photographs of works by Giotto, Duccio, Veronese, Grünewald, Rembrandt, de Hooch, Manet, and Matisse." Bearden says he substituted his "choice of colors for those of these artists, except for those of Manet and Matisse, when I was guided by color reproductions."[13]

Bearden's technique is as genuinely improvisational as that of Joe "Tricky Sam" Nanton, a trombonist in Ellington's band, who progressed through a laborious series of stages with his plunger mute in his effort to produce a "growl sound" that impersonates the human voice. Ellington also improvised; he used various combinations of players to create the sounds of instruments not in his own orchestra, or to duplicate with stunning authenticity the sounds of a passing train blowing its horn or beating its rhythms on the railroad tracks. Once, explaining how his creative process was related to jazz, Bearden alluded to the difficulty he faced in completing a painting based on Picasso's *Guitar Player*. While Bearden was at work on this painting, his friend Stuart Davis offered his advice: "You've got to look at varying things. Say you have people walking — you have to consider these things as musical beats; you don't want to have just dot dot dot dot." Bearden added that Davis saw color and form as wholly constitutive, a single artistic entity. He told Bearden: "Color has a place and it has a position."[14]

Later Bearden would say of his own use of color that he thought of the use of various shades and hues as similar to a musician's playing of counterpoint: "You put down one [color] and it calls for an answer. You have to look at it like a melody." Creating the "melody" is not limited to the choice of colors; placement and contextual positioning are also crucial. Bearden spoke of getting "something of that jazz feeling" in his abstract portrait of the jazz drummer Max Roach by using "horizontal lines of various colors." He manipulates colors to create "jazz feeling." He usually succeeds while others, in his view, sometimes fail. For instance, he criticizes the way certain French musicians play jazz, with a classical model as the controlling metaphor in their performance: "It seems to me that when I hear French jazz musicians play, that I can kind of tell. . . . There is a certain precision in the French — Descartes and the rest, even Seurat. Not like Van Gogh, who let himself go. A French musician doesn't want any surprises, like the ones you have to deal with in jazz."[15]

Bearden's reputation as a painter who employed improvisation persisted even after his death. Bearden allowed almost no one to watch him as he created his collages. Only his assistant, the artist André Thibault, saw Bearden create certain collages from start to finish. He speaks of what seemed to him a surprising technique,

Bearden's "flexibility with the dyes." Bearden often seemed to be "spilling" — adding too much of this or that color, and yet, Thibault says, the "drying process" usually created "striking imagery." The technique gave Bearden "freedom": "What always struck me about Romare's collages was that representation of total flexibility, total freedom in putting it down — and I don't mean the dyes or any other single technique in particular — I saw just how strongly he knew how to use color. He had total freedom in the use of color — unlike any other artist." [16]

Freedom and improvisation, though mutually dependent, are not equivalent in the creative process. Thibault concluded that Bearden, in a folksy American way, used his ingenuity in creating his collages. When Schwartzman asked whether Bearden gravitated "toward any color in particular," Thibault answered that Bearden used "whatever was at hand. . . . There were days we were picking through the garbage cans in the studio to find certain pieces of colored paper we needed. . . . Say we were left with just a blue and a green. Now combining those two pieces of paper, blue and green, and the dyes, we could make just about anything we wanted out of it. . . . [Bearden] was never thrown off creatively by the lack of a part. If we didn't have it at hand, he would make another part. And that's again the process of improvisation." Bearden told him, Thibault recalls, "that a great artist does not make mistakes: he just works them out." [17]

Bearden's process was familiar to Ralph Ellison. In their conversations (with or without Albert Murray) about art, literature, and jazz, he found in Bearden an artistic alter ego. He saw an unfolding personal analogy in his life and work, a no-nonsense lesson for his own creative struggles. In his essay "The Art of Romare Bearden" (written in 1968 at Murray's suggestion as the introduction to an exhibition catalogue for the State University of New York at Albany), Ellison praised Bearden and criticized other African American artists. Bearden, he wrote, expressed "the tragic predicament of his people without violating his passionate dedication to art as a fundamental and transcendent agency for confronting and revealing the world." [18]

The Black Aesthetic Movement epitomized Ellison's thinking regarding black artists who, unlike Bearden, were trapped within "a troublesome social anachronism." During the late 1960s, phrases such as black power, black pride, black culture helped to inspire racial solidarity and "self-determination" among African Americans. The literary equivalent was the Black Aesthetic Movement, led by writers and critics like Hoyt Fuller, editor of *Negro Digest* and later *Black World*, Leroi Jones, who changed his name to Amiri Baraka, and the critic Addison Gayle. Theirs was a call for "Black Poems" and "Black Art." In his catalogue essay Ellison writes: "Arising from an initial failure of social justice, . . . it [the anachronism] has had the damaging effect of alienating many Negro artists from the traditions, techniques, and theories indigenous to the arts through which they aspire to achieve themselves."[19] Ellison, himself the victim of scathing criticism for his presumed failure to write angry protest literature, maintained that many black visual artists, like their literary associates, had also limited themselves. Presumably these artists wanted to free themselves from what they considered to be restrictive European forms. Ellison considered this view anachronistic.

He chides "Negro artists" who, in contrast to Bearden, allow their fascination, "by the power of their anachronistic social imbalance," to truncate or thwart their creative impulses: "Indeed they take it as a major theme and focus for their attention, and they allow it to dominate their thinking about themselves, their people, their country and their art." Ellison celebrates "the true artist's" studied or "conscious concern with the most challenging possibilities of his form." Bearden seems to have accomplished precisely what Ellison sees as the "true" artist's difficult task. We should note here that Ellison's description of the true artist wholly fits his description of the true American writer: "As Bearden demonstrated here so powerfully, it is of the true artist's nature and mode of action to dominate all the world and time through technique and vision. His mission is to bring a new visual order into the world, and through his art he seeks to reset society's clock by imposing upon it his own method of defining the times. The urge to do this determines the form and the character of his social responsibility, spurs his restless exploration of plastic possibilities and accounts to a large extent for his creative aggressiveness."[20] Bearden's and Ellison's shared artistic and cultural assumptions echo in their statements and restatements of each other's thought. Responding in 1986 to a question from the artist Gwendolyn Wells, Bearden refers to the artist's inevitable struggle with "chaos." He alludes to Dante's *Inferno*: "The thing is, the artist confronts chaos. The whole thing of art is how do you organize chaos? . . . Dante, in his *Inferno*, meets Virgil after a while. He's lost and confused there, and Virgil says, 'I'll guide you, or take you through here.' . . . [He] is like the artist."[21]

Using Bearden's work as an exemplary standard of execution, Ellison raises a difficult question the "embattled" Negro artist is likely to ask: "How then . . . does an artist steeped in the most advanced lore of his craft and most passionately concerned about solving the more advanced problems of painting as *painting* address himself to the perplexing question of bringing his art to bear upon the task (never so urgent as now) of defining Negro American identity, and of pressing its claims for recognition and for justice?" He concludes that the artist feels "a near-unresolvable conflict between his urge to leave his mark upon the world through art and his ties to his group and its claims upon him."[22]

As early as the 1930s, in "The Negro Artist and Modern Art," Bearden, like Ellison, had harshly criticized the limitations of many Negro artists (he later modified his comments). He celebrates the fact that modern artists saw in African sculpture certain prototypical modernist ideals: "Of great importance has been the fact that the African would distort his figures, if by so doing he could achieve a more expressive form. This is one of the cardinal principles of the modern artist. . . . It is interesting to contrast the bold way in which the African sculptor approached his work, with the timidity of the Negro artist of today. His work is at best hackneyed and uninspired, and only rehashings from the work of an artist that might have influenced him. They have looked at nothing with their own eyes — seemingly content to use borrowed forms. They have evolved nothing original or native like the spiritual, or jazz music."[23]

Long before Bearden's exhibition was mounted at Albany, and before Ellison's rhapsodic praise of it, Bearden was thinking about the special problems he faced as a Negro artist. He mentions his photographic montages of the 1960s as dedicated attempts to save the image of the Negro from "becoming too much of an abstraction." He had tried to "establish a world through art in which the validity [of his] Negro experience could live and make its own logic."[24] Later he explained why he did not create propagandistic works during the heyday of the civil rights movement: "Naturally, I had strong feelings about the Civil Rights Movement, and about what was happening in the sixties," but, he said, "I have not created protest images. The world within the collage, if it is authentic, retains the right to speak for itself."[25]

Like Ellison, Bearden recognized no dichotomy between artistic expression and protest. He embraced any technique, tradition, or artist who could assist him in creating a vivid rendering of his subject, whether a group of slum dwellers or Odysseus returning home to Ithaca. International and European sources of inspiration and artistic instruction aided him in his renderings of Negro life. In his essay "Rectangular Structure in My Montage Paintings," he wrote: "It is not my aim to paint about the Negro in America in terms of propaganda. It is precisely my awareness of the distortions required of the polemicist that has caused me to paint the life of my people as I know it — as passionately and dispassionately as Breughel painted the life of the Flemish people of his day."[26]

In "The Art of Romare Bearden," Ellison does not mention Breughel's influence, although he refers to the influence on Bearden of the Mexican muralists Diego Rivera and José Orozco. He notes that Bearden had studied Giotto and de Hooch during the early 1940s. Bearden himself also recalled certain of his techniques that were inspired by Goya's paintings: "I've seen some of Goya's paintings where the underneath ground predominated over half the painting, and then he would . . . weave a certain blue color here and then develop those things that he wanted to be highlighted . . . an Italian technique from the Venetian painters —Tiepolo, Veronese, Tintoretto. . . . So I let the ground play through."[27] Ellison correctly notes the eclectic "artistic culture" from which Bearden derived his techniques. Ellison and Bearden believed that each artist's full engagement with the most advanced techniques and thinking of the times (as well as a necessary dedication to a catholicity of taste) remains a prerequisite for artistic mastery.

Bearden's artistic vision, exemplified by his use of blue in *The Piano Lesson*, reflects aspects of African American experience that extend beyond familiar stereotypes. Ellison says: "Bearden has sought . . . to reveal a world long hidden by the clichés of sociology and rendered cloudy by the distortions of newsprint and the false continuity imposed on our conception of Negro life by television and much documentary photography." Bearden "knows that the true complexity of the slum dweller and the tenant farmer requires a release from the prison of our media-dulled perception and a reassembling in forms which would convey something of the depth and wonder of the Negro American's stubborn humanity." [28] Such comments are a variation on some of Ellison's persistent themes — the role of "the true artist" and the complexity, the "depth and wonder," of African American experience. Ellison sees in Bearden's canvases and collages a vivid representation of his own artistic vision, just as he hears the voice of his own stories in Duke Ellington's "Black and Tan Fantasy" or "Harlem."

In 1961, Ellison told Richard G. Stern that "the marvelous" and "the terrible" are always present in Negro life. The inextricable union of those opposites represents the inherent nature of the human condition. With the restrictions and brutalities of segregation apparently on his mind, Stern had asked Ellison whether he would preserve "any specialized form of social life which makes for invidious distinctions." Referring to how "millions are damaged permanently" by segregation, he inquired whether Ellison would preserve "that which results in both the marvelous and the terrible," or, he wondered, whether "the marvelous should not endure while the terrible endures along with it." Ellison responded: "I think that the mixture of the marvelous and the terrible is a basic condition of human life, and that the persistence of human ideals represents the marvelous pulling itself up out of the chaos of the universe." He wished to preserve some of the "precious" elements of Negro experience acquired through "the harsh discipline of Negro life": "I speak of the faith, the patience, the humor, the sense of timing, the rugged sense of life and the manner of expressing it which all go to define the American Negro." [29]

Bearden, Ellison believed, understood "the harsh discipline" and recorded both the marvelous and the terrible in colorful variations. His paintings of Harlem street scenes and slum dwellers have resonance and meaning beyond immediate and local circumstances. Ellison concludes that Bearden's "combination of techniques is in itself eloquent of the sharp breaks, leaps in consciousness, distortions, paradoxes, reversals, telescoping of time and surreal blending of styles, values, hopes and dreams which characterize much of Negro American history." [30]

Shared Assumptions: Albert Murray
Riffs on the Marvelous, the Terrible, and
the Heroic in African American Culture

In 1994, Louis Edwards had an exchange with Murray about his relationship to Bearden and Ellison:

Edwards: Let's talk a little bit about Romare Bearden. . . .
Murray: I had known about Bearden's work on my own, but I
    also knew of Bearden's work through Ralph [Ellison]. In
    fact, in [my daughter's] room there's a painting which
    Bearden originally gave to Ralph. Ralph gave it to me be-
    cause he ran out of space, and then I was instrumental in
    his getting a *bigger* Bearden painting when I got him to do
    [his essay] on Bearden for the Albany exhibition. . . . But by
    this time I was Bearden's chief literary advisor, so to speak.
    We [Bearden and I] collaborated on most of his stuff.
Edwards: When you say collaborate, what do you mean?
Murray: Frames of reference and titles. He'd say, "Well, *we're*
    gonna do a one-man show." And then I'd say, "We oughta
    do something on jazz." And Bearden would say, "What
    should I do?" . . . I met him in 1950. . . . We saw each other
    on an even more regular basis than Ellison and I did, al-
    though Ellison and I talked on the phone a lot. Romy and I
    would get together and we would go and look at all these
    paintings. That would have started in 1963, when I moved
    to New York and got back in touch with him. . . . And we
    used to meet at Books & Company because a friend of ours
    had started it. We would meet over there every Saturday and
    we would hold court. . . . Meanwhile, I'd be setting up the
    outline and naming the paintings. He would say, "What
    should I do now?" [31]

Murray also believes that some of Bearden's works, his "urban-
scapes," are the artistic equivalents of Duke Ellington's composi-
tions. Murray concludes that Bearden's paintings titled *The Block, The
Street, Evening Lenox Avenue, The Dove, Rocket to the Moon,* and *Black Man-
hattan* resemble Ellington's "tone parallels and celebrations," such as
"Uptown Downbeat," "Echoes of Harlem," "I'm Slapping Seventh
Avenue with the Sole of My Shoe," "Drop Me Off in Harlem," and
"Harlem Airshaft." [32] Bearden's and Ellington's representations of

Harlem capture its paradoxes — including the marvelous and the terrible.

The sense one gets of Murray, a college football and basketball player and retired Air Force major, as a renaissance man and jazz aficionado is revealed by his world of photographs and artifacts. Calling the items in Murray's Harlem apartment "two-dimensional products of a vigorously three-dimensional life," Mark Feeney writes of a "dreamy snapshot" of Ralph Ellison taken by Murray at a picnic during the 1930s. Feeney says: "In another picture, Murray confers with James Baldwin in Paris in 1950. Other photos show Murray backstage with Duke Ellington, between sets with Count Basie, greeting Wynton Marsalis. There are letters from Ellison, Robert Penn Warren, Langston Hughes, Joseph Campbell— and one from a former White House aide, recounting how he overheard an appreciative Lyndon Johnson read aloud the appraisal of LBJ in Murray's book *South to a Very Old Place*."[33] Feeney calls Murray "one of the planet's champion talkers." He notices that Murray's bookshelves are "filled with first editions of Hemingway and Faulkner, Thomas Mann and T. S. Eliot, André Malraux and W. H. Auden." He reports that Auden is "a particular favorite" and that Murray "will emphasize points by quoting from memory snatches of his poetry, as well as passages from Edna St. Vincent Millay, e. e. cummings, and Marianne Moore. The words tumble out as if part of an endless tutorial."[34]

In "The Function of the Heroic Image," Murray provides a succinct overview of the assumptions and intellectual point of view underpinning his books. Even a cursory look reveals how closely his thought parallels that of Ellison's and Bearden's. He says that *The Omni-Americans: New Perspectives on Black Experience and American Culture* (1970), his first book, grew out of his "reaction to the ever-so-popular oversimplifications of the so-called social sciences." His is a scathing critique of social scientists and their comments on race. He eschews their categorical thinking about "races" and writes: "There's no social scientist in the United States that can define what is black and what is white. . . . No such definition is possible. And yet you've had survey after survey after survey, which divides people and draws conclusions based on 'racial differences.' "[35] Murray, like Ellison, turns to literature, "the human discipline," as Murray calls it, with its "great minds" and "marvelous metaphors." He says: "I know the vital statistics. I *know the facts. But I'm looking for something better.* And that something better is a story of the possibility of glory on earth" (italics his).[36]

Murray's focus on "marvelous metaphors" and the "possibility of glory" in human affairs is analogous to Ellison's sense of *transcendence,* whether in the story of the triumphant vindication of an individual like Frederick Douglass or a race and nation, as in the Supreme Court's affirmative vote in 1954 on the Brown decision. For Murray, Ellison, and Bearden, *transcendence* also refers to the rendering of the human experience by the artist — writer, musician, painter, or any artist — in its multifaceted ugliness and beauty. Murray says he strives to write about "heroic action." This theme connects him to both Bearden and Ellison. Each sees in great literature dramatic renditions of transcendent truths and heroic possibility.[37] "But literature teaches us that mankind has always defined itself *against* the negatives thrown it by both society and the universe," Ellison observes. "It is human will, human hope, and human effort which make the difference. Let's not forget that the great tragedies not only treat of negative matters, of violence, brutalities, defeats, but they treat them within a context of man's will to act, to challenge reality and to snatch triumph from the teeth of destruction." [38]

One sees in Murray's writings other dimensions and characterizations of heroic action. For instance, Murray plays a sustained variation on Ellison's notion of the heroic human will in *South to a Very Old Place* (1971), his second book, which he calls "a sort of nonfiction or documentary novel." Instead of coming back from his journey south with a "sociological report or a bunch of journalistic bullshit," Murray brought back "a metaphor about the imperatives of heroic action." He says his experience, along with that of the people who grew up with him, had taught him "to take on the responsibility of saviors, of Prometheus, of bringing light, of bringing fire, bringing enlightenment." Like Ellison and Bearden, he protests the categorical depiction of African Americans as mere victims. Murray considers such portraiture to be as reductive in life as it is in art. He says that his vision "had nothing to do with being a victim. It had to do with the fact that if you were faced with a problem, the problem was a dragon and you were the hero. So you had to forge a sword and find out how to rip at the scales." [39]

Murray also shares with Ellison what the former calls a central concept of his writing, his sense of the role "antagonistic cooperation" plays in the dynamics of heroic action. Ellison explicitly refers to antagonistic cooperation in "The World and the Jug," his 1960s exchange with Irving Howe. Murray extends Ellison's definition of the way in which apparent intellectual adversaries aid and abet each other's thinking in the interest of a more precise record for all. He explores the concept in *The Hero and the Blues* (1973), his third book. Murray says that the concept is "at the center of all stories," explaining that "it means that you can't be a saint . . . unless there's some sin for you to avoid. You can't be a surgeon unless you have disease that you can operate on. . . . You can't be a great hitter unless there are great pitchers. You can't be a champion unless you have great challengers. . . . You can't have a hero without a dragon." [40]

Murray, like Ellison, views the blues as a heroic and life-sustaining form. "As a form," Ellison asserts in "Richard Wright's Blues" (1945), "the blues is an autobiographical chronicle of a personal catastrophe expressed lyrically." In *Stomping the Blues* (1976), Murray echoes Ellison: "What it [the blues] all represents is an attitude toward the nature of human experience . . . that is both elemental and comprehensive. It is a statement about confronting the complexities inherent in the human situation and about improvising or experimenting and riffing or otherwise playing with (or even gambling with) such possibilities as are also inherent in the obstacles, the disjunctures, and the jeopardy. It is also a statement about perseverance and about resilience and thus all about the maintenance of equilibrium despite precarious circumstances and about achieving elegance in the very process of coping with the rudiments of subsistence." [41]

Murray shares with Ellison and Bearden an abiding faith in the power of great literature and art as well as a dedication to the achievement and expression of elegance and truth. For him, jazz and the jazz musician are central to his "whole literary, philosophical system of American Identity." [42] The discussion of jazz and the avid collecting of jazz recordings were ongoing activities for both Murray and Ellison. In their correspondence Murray encourages Ellison to write about Jimmy Rushing, and Ellison suggests to Murray that he write and clarify certain aspects of the blues. They share and trade ideas on a range of topics, and they are usually in agreement. [43] There are moments in his essays and interviews on jazz when Ellison provides a sharply focused note upon which Murray extends and elaborates. Take, for instance, Murray's reflections on Armstrong and Ellington.

In *The Blue Devils of Nada*, Murray shows how Ellington was able to make his music by focusing on a period (during the 1950s) in Paris when he and Louis Armstrong had been commissioned to play for a movie being shot there. The movie, *Paris Blues*, starred Paul Newman, Sidney Poitier, Diahann Carroll, and Joanne Woodward. Armstrong appeared onscreen as a famous trumpeter, but Ellington had been commissioned to compose and conduct an original score and to provide new arrangements for his "Mood Indigo" and "Sophisticated Lady," as well as for Billy Strayhorn's "Take the A Train."

Both Armstrong and Ellington were familiar with Hollywood on and off camera. Armstrong had appeared in productions such as *Pennies from Heaven, Going Places, A Midsummer Night's Dream, Cabin in the Sky,* and *High Society*. The year before being asked to write the score for *Paris Blues*, Ellington had created the background music for Otto Preminger's *Anatomy of a Murder* (1959) and he "had made his screen debut decades before as a composer and also as a leader and performer in a musical short titled *Black and Tan*." [44]

In *Stomping the Blues* (1976), Murray refers to the old saying — "It don't mean a thing if it ain't got that swing" — that Ellington set to music and explains how Ellington extended Armstrong's "aesthetic point of view." Murray calls Armstrong "a Promethean bringer of syncopated lightning from the land of the Titans," and adds, "Ellington, whose music embodies among other things the most comprehensive synthesis of Armstrong's innovations, was declaring that for most intents and purposes the Armstrong principle was universal." [45]

Murray considers Ellington the apotheosis of American genius, America's musical equivalent to Shakespeare. He describes the longevity and stunning range of the composer's career: "Ellington is without question jazz's most productive composer-arranger. Ellington wrote more than two thousand compositions and arranged and rearranged many of them." [46] Murray focuses upon Ellington's work habits and his intense creativity in a review of the composer's autobiography, *Music Is My Mistress*, explaining that for Ellington, "in whom the instrumentalist, composer, and conductor were so totally and inextricably interrelated, performing music was absolutely indispensable to writing it." Ellington was never far from a piano or keyboard. Murray observes: "Not only was there always a keyboard instrument of some kind in his dressing room whenever space permitted, such was also the case with his hotel suites and even his hospital rooms. And he was forever noodling, and doodling and jotting and dotting no matter who else was there and what else was going on." [47] Two significant images are superimposed in Murray's brief sketch. There is Ellington the obsessive composer, dedicated to the perfection of his craft. His "mistress," symbolized by the ever-present keyboard, must always be kept near. There is as well Ellington the hardworking American, going beyond the call of duty.

When Murray turns to an analysis of how Ellington works with his orchestra, he describes a unique manner of composing, the inseparable aspects of Ellington as "instrumentalist, composer and conductor." Ellington "seldom finished scoring his music until he had heard it played back not only on the appropriate instrument, but also by the individual musician he had in mind. . . . What he actually did, of course, was to play a composition into the desired shape and texture during rehearsal. . . . It was . . . a way of continuing the process of creation and orchestration that he had begun on the piano some time before." Ellington, as a performing composer, uses his whole orchestra as "a personal instrument" to a greater degree than most conductors: "He not only set tempos, moods, and voicing as if the various sections of the orchestra were physical extensions of the keyboard, but he also inserted riffs and dictated phrasings, shadings and even revisions." [48] Murray's careful account of Ellington at work appears to contradict stories of the musician's spontaneous moments of creativity. It was with this vast experience as a performing composer that he managed to write it down or make it up as he went along as though transcribing notes from music he heard in the air.

The complex and multidimensional evocation of Harlem one gets in Bearden's paintings like The Block or The Street, or in Ellington's tone parallels like "Echoes of Harlem" and "Harlem Airshaft," is usually missing in sociological studies and essays. Murray's sense of the heroic tradition in African American culture led him to call the usual and stereotypical view of Harlem "welfare department tear-jerk rhetoric." James Baldwin's first published essay, "The Harlem Ghetto," is representative of what Murray has in mind. In contrast to Ellison's, Bearden's, and Murray's paradoxical visions of Harlem, Baldwin wrote only of a disheartened place: "Harlem, physically at least, has changed very little in my parents' lifetime or in mine. Now as then the buildings are old and in desperate need of repair, the streets are crowded and dirty, there are too many human beings per square block. . . . All over Harlem now there is felt the same bitter expectancy with which, in my childhood, we awaited winter: It is coming and it will be hard; there is nothing anyone can do about it."[49] When Baldwin moves from his physical description to his psychological assessment of the consequences of Harlem's deterioration, he says: "All of Harlem is pervaded by a sense of congestion, rather like the insistent, maddening, claustrophobic pounding in the skull that comes from trying to breathe in a very small room with all the windows shut."[50]

Baldwin was only twenty-three when "The Harlem Ghetto," his first significant essay, was published in *Commentary* in 1948. In later essays and fictional scenes of Harlem he, too, would capture some of the "marvelous," although his mood and rhetorical style, especially in his autobiographical essays, remained anguished and melancholy. In *The Omni-Americans*, Murray criticizes Baldwin's vision of Harlem as it emerges specifically in Baldwin's third novel, *Another Country*. Murray writes: "Nor does he [Baldwin] account for its [Harlem's] universally celebrated commitment to elegance in motion, to colorful speech idioms, to high style, not only in personal deportment but even in handling mechanical devices. . . . Much of what he says denies the very existence of Harlem's fantastically knowing satire, its profound awareness and rejection of so much that is ridiculous in downtown doings. Sometimes, he writes as though he had never heard the comedians at the Apollo Theatre." Murray concludes that in "The Harlem Ghetto" Baldwin focuses on "the material plight of Harlem," not its full "life."[51]

Murray's assessment of Harlem is reminiscent of Ellison's catalogue of wonders in the Oklahoma City of his boyhood days. Murray's comments do not suggest that either Ellison or Bearden missed or deliberately ignored the human pain and suffering of Harlem's or Oklahoma City's mean streets. But Murray shares their more positive assumptions, seeing in Ellison's and Bearden's works blacks rendered in all of their human dimensions. Unlike Baldwin, they do not see the dwellers of Harlem or other blacks in the United States as living lives wholly separate from the general circumstances, cultural attitudes, and institutional values of other Americans.

In "Harlem Is Nowhere," one of Ellison's earliest essays, written in 1948 — the same year in which Baldwin's "The Harlem Ghetto" was published — Ellison attempts to puzzle out the fundamental situation of blacks in New York. "Harlem Is Nowhere" shows a developing young writer applauding the white psychiatrist, Dr. Frederic Wertham, who had established, primarily for Harlem blacks, the Lafargue Psychiatric Clinic. Ellison notes that the clinic "rejects all stereotypes" and situates the black American "as a member of a racial and cultural minority, as an American citizen caught in certain political and economic relationships, and as a modern man living in a revolutionary world." [52] In this piece, written four years before the publication of Invisible Man, Ellison is already attempting to correct the typical characterization of African American personality.

But Ellison's portrayal of Harlem itself, though different from Baldwin's in its rhetoric, recalls a similarly stark view: "To live in Harlem is to dwell in the very bowels of the city, it is to pass a labyrinthine existence among streets that explode monotonously skyward with the spires and crosses of churches and clutter underfoot with garbage and decay. Harlem is a ruin; many of its ordinary aspects (its crime, casual violence, crumbling buildings with littered areaways, ill-smelling halls and vermin-invaded rooms) are indistinguishable from the distorted images that appear in dreams, and which like muggers haunting a lonely hall, quiver in the waking mind with hidden and threatening significance." [53]

Ellison is perhaps searching to explain the living conditions that drove many of Lafargue's clients into mental illness. He shows us the source of the colloquialism "Harlem is nowhere." Ellison takes us momentarily out of Baldwin's claustrophobic winter room with its closed window. The "streets explode monotonously skyward with the spires and crosses of churches." The crosses are primarily ironic symbols rather than redemptive beckonings, but the church spires still point upward, even with the sky as an indifferent witness, toward the ultimate symbol of transcendence, heaven.

Ellison recognizes that while Harlemites may "dwell in the very bowels of the city," a permanent symbol of the invisible and ambiguous position of blacks that characterizes his work, there is still the possibility of transcendence: "For if Harlem is the scene of the folk-Negro's death agony, it is also the setting of his transcendence. Here it is possible for talented youths to leap through the development of decades in a brief twenty years, while beside them white-haired adults crawl in the feudal darkness of their childhood. . . . Here the grandchildren of those who possessed no written literature examine their lives through the eyes of Freud and Marx, Kierkegaard and Kafka, Malraux and Sartre. It explains the nature of a world so fluid and shifting that often within the mind the real and the unreal merge, and the marvelous beckons from behind the same sordid reality that denies its existence." [54]

Ellison's discussion of Harlem, while seeming at first to duplicate Baldwin's, takes us beyond the image of Harlem as merely a bleak place. Ellison's Harlem remains a part of New York City, a city of American dreams — of shattered dreams and dreams deferred, but also of dreams come true. For example, when Ellison speaks of his own arrival in New York in 1936, and looks backward almost four decades after writing "Harlem Is Nowhere," he says: "The very idea of being in New York was dreamlike, for like many young Negroes of the time, I thought of it as the freest of American cities, and considered Harlem as the site and symbol of Afro-American progress and hope. Indeed I was young and bookish enough to think of Manhattan as my substitute for Paris, and of Harlem as a place of Left Bank excitement." [55] Of course, Baldwin had grown up in Harlem, and to him it was hardly a dream.

Ellison's sense of Harlem is, in the end, Ellisonian. Like Bearden, he makes it over in his own image. Murray concludes: "Whatever Ellington played became Ellington, as whatever Picasso painted became a Picasso beyond all else. And the same is true — and has been for some time now — of Romare Bearden. When one looks at his paintings one sees more than the subject matter. Ultimately it is not only Bearden's North Carolina or Bearden's Harlem or Bearden's musicians or Bearden's Odysseus, but also a Bearden stylization of an attitude toward human existence, a Bearden statement/counterstatement and thus that which stands for Bearden himself, and hence a Bearden." [56] Whatever Ellison wrote about became Ellisonian. Harlem was one of his favorite subjects. It was also one of Murray's and Bearden's.

In fact, Harlem is the subject of The Block, Bearden's largest painting. Calvin Tomkins explains its genesis: "Standing on the terrace of Albert Murray's apartment, on West 132nd Street, one day in 1971, looking across at the rows of four-story buildings that make up the block on Lenox Avenue between 132nd and 133rd, Bearden conceived the idea for his largest painting. The Block is actually six pictures joined together making an eighteen-foot work. . . . It shows not only the street and the houses but also (shades of [Bearden's childhood friend] Eugene) the rooms behind the façades, where people are eating, bathing, making love, attending church (the block has two churches), getting their hair cut — just going about the ordinary business of life. The feeling conveyed is one of celebration." [57]

Ellison explains what Bearden captures in The Block: "In brief, Bearden has used (and most playfully) all of his artistic knowledge and skill to create a curve of plastic vision which reveals to us something of the mysterious complexity of those who dwell in our urban slums. But his is the eye of a painter, not that of a sociologist, and here the elegant architectural details . . . exist in a setting of gracious but neglected streets and the buildings in which the hopeful and the hopeless live cheek by jowl, where failed human wrecks and the confidently expectant explorers of the frontiers of human possibility are crowded together." [58]

Murray refers to Bearden's "stylization of an attitude." This phrase captures what these three artist-intellectuals were all about. Given racial presumptions and prejudices, they had to maintain a remarkable discipline and faith in their mutually shared sense of aesthetic and personal possibility. In 1950–51 (just before the publication of Invisible Man), Murray and Ellison exchanged a series of letters about their future as literary men. Murray was still in the Air Force and was teaching (as an English and ROTC instructor) at Tuskegee Institute in Alabama. He had recently returned from his first trip to Europe and was hard at work on his first book. In November 1950, he writes Ellison to report on his teaching schedule, which includes "Composition and the Theory of Literature" and "English Lit. Survey," and says: "And I can think fairly clearly here even though almost nobody else can or wants to or has any interest at all in what I'm doing." Murray understands and accepts the lack of interest in his literary aspirations. He informs Ellison: "By this time, you have seen the Faulkner story in the October issue of Harper's. The whole issue is worth having, I think. So far, I have not been able to do much reading this fall, but who wants to be reading when at last he has something to write? However, I'm going through the books I brought back from Paris — and, by the way, I think that my French is continuing to improve. I'm still working at it every day." [59]

In June of 1951, Ellison writes Murray to inform him that he has completed *Invisible Man*. He and Albert Erskine, his editor, are "preparing it for the printer, who should have it in July or August." He tells Murray that perhaps both of them will have books published in the same year. Moreover, he makes comments that sum up the aesthetic point of view to which he remains faithful to the end: "Come to think of it writing novels must surely be an upset to somebody's calculations. Tuskegee certainly wasn't intended for that. But more important, I believe that we'll offer some demonstration of the rich and untouched possibilities offered by Negro life for imaginative treatment. I'm sick to my guts of reading stuff like the piece by Richard Gibson in the *Kenyon Review*. He's complaining that Negro writers are expected to write like Wright, Himes, Hughes, which he thinks is unfair because, by God, *he's* read Gide! Yes, and Proust and a bunch of them advance guard European men of letters. . . . If he thinks he's the black Gide why doesn't he write and prove it? . . . Then all the rest of us would fade away before the triumph of pure, abstract homosexual art over life. . . . No, I think you're doing it the right way. You've written a book out of your own vision of life, and when it is read the reader will see *and feel* that you have indeed read Gide and Malraux, Mann and whoever the hell else had something to say to you — including a few old Mobile hustlers and whore ladies, no doubt." [60]

In the same letter, Ellison summarizes what he had tried to achieve in *Invisible Man*: "Erskine's having a time deciding what kind of novel it is, and I can't help him. For me it's just a big fat ole Negro lie, meant to be told during cotton picking time over a water bucket full of corn [whiskey], with a dipper passing back and forth at a good fast clip so that no one, not even the narrator himself, will realize how utterly preposterous the lie actually is. I just hope someone points out that aspect of it." [61]

In using "lie" Ellison means hyperbole or verbal extravagance. He is also specifically alluding to African American humor, which works in *Invisible Man* and the culture at large as an antidote to racial provocation and prejudice. Bearden and Murray shared Ellison's viewpoint on the general role of the African American artist. They all maintained that serious art about African Americans should reflect the artist's own original vision. Furthermore, they believed that any artist — whether painter, musician, or writer — should, if necessary, beg, borrow, and even steal various artistic techniques that would enable that artist to make his or her own vision articulate and unique.

Jazz Underground
Invisible Man as Jazz Text

Ellison gave our age a new metaphor for social alienation. His definition of "invisibility" is so common now, so much a part of the culture and language — like a coin handled by billions — that it is automatically invoked when we talk about the situation of American blacks, and for any social group we willingly refuse to see.

— Charles Johnson, introduction to Invisible Man, 1994 edition

Invisible Man as Jazz Text

Invisible Man is a retrospective and episodic tale. Sequestered in a Harlem cellar, Ellison's nameless narrator often referred to as Invisible Man, a young intellectual for whom an unexamined life has little attraction, reflects upon the bewildering consequences of his actions. He starts out fighting in a black battle staged for the sadistic amusement of the important white men in his southern hometown. He survives an explosion in the basement of a paint factory, and during his subsequent hospitalization he narrowly avoids a prefrontal lobotomy. He protests eloquently when an elderly black couple is evicted from their Harlem apartment. He is exploited by a Communist-style organization, the Brotherhood. His friend Tod Clifton is shot to death by a white cop.

A race riot breaks out in Harlem after Clifton's death, and Invisible Man escapes an angry mob of militant blacks determined to hang him. He ends up in a Harlem cellar, playing his phonograph and listening to Louis Armstrong singing "What Did I Do to Be So Black and Blue": "Sometimes now I listen to Louis while I have my favorite dessert of vanilla ice cream and sloe gin. I pour the red liquid over the white mound, watching it glisten and the vapor rising as Louis bends that military instrument into a beam of lyrical sound. Perhaps I like Louis Armstrong because he's made poetry out of being invisible. I think it must be because he's unaware that he *is* invisible." [1]

To Invisible Man, the sound of Louis Armstrong singing is both a source of inspiration and entertainment. He wants to *"feel"* the music's vibration with his ear and his "whole body." Indeed the music helps gratify all of his senses. Armstrong's playing of "What Did I Do to Be So Black and Blue" is associated with Invisible Man's favorite dessert, allowing Ellison to underscore the sweet American originality of Armstrong's sound. The patriotic colors — the white ice cream, the red sloe gin, the transmuted blue notes of Armstrong's voice and horn — amount to a prelude for the novel.

If, as Ellison envisions it, American culture is "jazz-shaped," *Invisible Man* reflects the musical process and form of democratic culture. Yet neither Ellison's novel nor his essays appear obviously experimental or improvisational. Unlike writers who are relentlessly innovative, such as Jack Kerouac and William Burroughs, Ellison attempts to achieve a jazz-inspired rendition of Jamesian virtuosity. But Jamesian aesthetics is his starting point rather than his end. He strives to take the American novel beyond the achievement of James, Melville, Stowe, Faulkner, and Wright by including and exploring the ambiguous presence and vernacular energy — the speech, accents, faith, and wild humor — of African Americans.

The genesis of the novel is related to a joke Ellison heard a comedian tell at Harlem's famed Apollo Theatre on 125th Street. In his introduction to the Franklin Mint edition of *Invisible Man*, Ellison says that the opening line — "I am an invisible man" — came to him and would not go away. Frustrated, he pulled the page from the typewriter and crumpled it. Later, Ellison recalled a voice: "And suddenly I could hear in my head a blackface comedian bragging on the stage of Harlem's Apollo Theatre to the effect that each generation of his family had become so progressively black of complexion that no one, not even its own mother, had ever been able to see the two-year-old baby. The audience had roared with laughter, and I recognized something of the same joking, in-group Negro American irony sounding from my rumpled page." [2]

Ellison has directly addressed his use of jazz aesthetics in *Invisible Man*. In 1965, Richard Kostelanetz asked him, "Would you say then analogously your book is to Western literature as jazz is to Western music?" Ellison responded: "Yes, I would just point out that they are both Western, they are both American precisely because they try to use any and everything which has been developed by great music and great literature. As for music, on the other hand, I suspect that the one body of music which expresses the United States — which expresses this continent — is jazz and blues."[3]

Invisible Man is a jazz text. Though true to specific historical incidents, it rearranges them in highly imaginative ways. It consciously riffs upon or plays countless variations on familiar literary and cultural themes. It raises questions and reflects upon topics suggested by other writers such as Melville and Emerson; events such as the Harlem riot of summer 1943; and historical personages such as Frederick Douglass and Abraham Lincoln. Its most radical and innovative jazz moments are those in which the narrator takes us on philosophical flights of fancy concerning the arduous task of being an American and an American writer. At such moments, one can hear and see in Ellison's virtuosity lightning-like flashes of a point of view so ironic as to border on the subversive. Other critics have noted Ellison's imaginative riffs but have paid scant attention to his solo flights, his philosophical and descriptive cadenzas.

Eric Sundquist writes that Ellison's novel constructs history as if it were "a jazz composition or performance." History in Invisible Man is "a form of subjective temporality — a constructed story, not a set of objective facts." He concludes: "His intricate individual variations, or riffs, on motifs or images, as well as the protagonist's self-evident improvisation of new identities in a spiraling series of new circumstances, are lesser elements of the book's grander design, which narrates the course of modern African-American life in the nameless protagonist's experiences."[4]

Sundquist makes a convincing point. The story, after all, is told after the fact. Time present is actually remembered time past. The narrator, by now mature and highly conscious, decides, like an autobiographer, who and what comes next. He permits certain characters—Rev. Homer Barbee, Mr. Norton, Jim Trueblood, Bledsoe, Lucius Brockway, Mary Rambo, Tarp, Sybil, Tod Clifton, Ras the Exhorter — to tell their own stories, take their bows, and exit. Thereafter, he occasionally alludes to them, but they rarely reappear. Each of these characters, like so many players in a jazz performance, takes his or her cues from the narrator. Some, like Jim Trueblood, take long solos. Others, like Brother Tarp, tell their stories with sensational brevity. Some characters, like the mad vet who calls Invisible Man "a walking personification of the negative," voice revelatory moments of counterpoint. Finally, Invisible Man himself offers his own series of speeches — an earnest high-school valedictory address, an inspired and spontaneous oration after witnessing the eviction of the old Harlem couple, a eulogy for fellow Brotherhood member Tod Clifton. His curtain speech is his muted trumpeting of democratic ideals and artistic angst in the epilogue.

Invisible Man is also a book of sounds and "signifying." In his study The Signifying Monkey: A Theory of African-American Literary Criticism, Henry Louis Gates, Jr., calls Invisible Man a "talking book." Ellison's book, like others by African American writers, helped "to establish a collective black voice through the sublime example of an individual text, and thereby to register a black presence in letters."[5] Gates does not specify Invisible Man as his "sublime example," but he provides clear reasons to read it as exemplary. Published at the midpoint of the twentieth century, Invisible Man is the "talking book," the "sublime example," because it speaks so eloquently across two centuries and seeks to address the fundamental unity in the diversity of American life.

In 1981, as the novel approached its thirtieth anniversary, Ellison added a long introduction in which he says, "So my task was one of revealing the human universals hidden within the plight of one who was both black and American, . . . as a way of dealing with the sheer rhetorical challenge involved in communicating across our barriers of race and religion, class, color and region. . . . I would have to . . . give him [Invisible Man] a consciousness in which serious philosophical questions could be raised, provide him with a range of diction that could play upon the richness of our readily shared vernacular speech and construct a plot that would bring him in contact with a variety of American types as they operated on various levels of society."[6] In its use of modes of black vernacular speech, rhetoric, and song — spirituals, blues, folk tales, sermons, popular lyrics — Invisible Man "talks" to and exploits an array of black voices and sounds, incorporating and celebrating indigenous American culture. In fact, the novel is like New York City, its primary setting — loud. It is an extravaganza of sounds — various voices, idioms, and accents surfacing here and there, sermons, speeches, folk rhymes, advertising slogans, profanities shouted on Harlem streets.

Yet *Invisible Man* represents considerably more than its inventive melding of the oral and the written in the African American literary tradition. Nor does the novel limit itself to an engaging conversation with African American and American literature. It assumes oracular authority, looking back at midcentury through world literature and history, riffing on various ideas and books. Like the jazz virtuoso who takes familiar themes and techniques from classical and popular traditions to make them strange and new, Ellison appropriates and improvises upon genres such as the picaresque novel and uses modernist techniques like the flashback, interior monologue, and stream of consciousness.

Invisibility Blues

Invisible Man interprets the American experience — with subplots related to democracy, race, and technology — as one of the grand narratives in world history. Invisibility, Ellison's modernist theme, characterizes the anonymity of modern life. Each person counts as a mere face or body in a city crowd where nobody knows names and there is no place to call home. In his introduction to *New Essays on Invisible Man*, Robert O'Meally addresses this point: "Invisibility is a metaphor that has moved from its original literary context to become a key metaphor for its era."[7] Ellison's metaphor includes but is hardly limited to African Americans, though it speaks in an immediate way to the black American's historical situation. In that light, *Invisible Man* has precursors, especially James Weldon Johnson's *Autobiography of an Ex-Colored Man* (1900) and W. E. B. Du Bois's *Souls of Black Folk* (1903). Ellison's plot — including the nameless narrator's quest for identity and self-understanding — echoes that of Johnson's novel. But unlike Johnson's nameless narrator, Ellison's character does not pass for white. He is, after all, too dark, but he does "hibernate" in a Harlem cellar, his identity sheltered from public scrutiny.

The *Souls of Black Folk* hints at the phenomenon of invisibility, but a crucial difference exists. In a famous passage Du Bois defines "double consciousness" and emphasizes the Negro's twoness: "two souls, two thoughts, two unreconciled strivings, two warring ideals in one dark body, whose dogged strength alone keeps it from being torn asunder." [8] Du Bois refers to "a peculiar sensation . . . this sense of always looking at one's self through the eyes of others, of measuring one's soul by the tape of a world that looks on in amused contempt and pity." In another work, *Dusk of Dawn* (1940), Du Bois describes what he calls "the psychological meaning of caste segregation." He writes: "It is as though one, looking out from a dark cave in a side of a mountain, sees the world passing and speaks to it; . . . showing them. . . . It gradually penetrates the minds of the prisoners that the people passing do not hear; that some thick sheet of invisible but horribly tangible plate glass is between them and the world." [9] Ellison, writing years after Du Bois, also focuses on the onlooker, the source of "the amused contempt and pity." *Invisible Man* foreshadows considerations of the "gaze" and identity as "social construction." Invisible Man — seemingly oblivious to his "double consciousness" — perceives the social absurdity of his position. He does not call it the "male gaze" or the "white gaze," but emphasizes sight and misperception: "That invisibility to which I refer occurs because of a peculiar disposition of the eyes of those with whom I come in contact. A matter of the construction of their *inner* eyes, those eyes with which they look through their physical eyes upon reality." Invisible Man seems almost unconcerned about the "contempt" of the looker. He says at the end of the passage: "It is sometimes advantageous to be unseen." [10]

Invisibility, as the narrator defines it, is tied to the search for identity. Invisible Man is like a young jazzman trying to come into his own. In "The Golden Age, Time Past," Ellison says that the jazzman must " 'find himself,' must be reborn, must find . . . his soul. All this through achieving that subtle identification between his instrument and his deepest drives which will allow him to express his own unique ideas and his own unique voice. He must achieve, in short, his self-determined identity." [11]

Notes Underground

As Invisible Man finds his way, Ellison allows characters such as Jim Trueblood, Lucius Brockway, and Brother Tarp to tell their own stories in their own words, as though taking turns at solos. Each character's story embodies the complex past of African Americans. Their stories, the sounds of their individual voices—their vernacular expressions and witty remarks — highlight Ellison's way, à la jazz, of moving the narrative along. The novel alternates between Invisible Man's long discursive vamps and the other characters' solos, brief or extended. The characters, anonymous in official histories, voice their own triumphs and defeats, educating Invisible Man.

Invisible Man's journey leads him to revelatory moments. His encounter with Lucius Brockway in the Liberty Paints factory, for instance, suggests a staged American ritual of self-discovery. Invisible Man tells us the story: "Flags were fluttering in a breeze from each of a maze of buildings below the [paint factory] sign, and for a moment it was like watching some vast patriotic ceremony from a distance."[12] The narrator is instructed to put drops — "glistening black drops" — of "black dope" into the paint mixture in order to produce the company's famous "optic white." This Ellisonian scene symbolizes the vital presence of blacks in both the making and preservation of American culture. When Invisible Man confuses the crucial ingredient, the black drops, with concentrated paint remover, he is abruptly transferred to another building, where he meets Lucius Brockway, a white-haired black employee well past retirement age and fearful of being replaced. Ellison heightens the power of this scene by giving Lucius Brockway, apparently an invisible man in the company's hierarchy, extraordinary power underground. Brockway controls the production of the vital black drops. Furthermore, he has played a definitive role in the company's development and success from its inception.

Invisible Man finds Brockway in "a deep basement . . . three levels underground." In colorful vernacular speech, Brockway tells his story: "Everybody knows I been here ever since there's been a here — even helped dig the first foundation."[13] Hidden from public view and at the literal bottom of the company, he is, in fact, wholly different from what he appears to be. Brockway's comments represent something larger than his own vernacular expression of his position. Ellison turns the basement of Liberty Paints into a symbolic stage for the drama of American democracy. Brockway's position is figuratively similar to that of Jefferson Davis Randolph — a black custodian who was Ellison's deeply influential "adopted grandfather." Randolph worked in the law library of the Oklahoma State Capitol and, according to Ellison, was often consulted on points of law by the white legislators.[14] Brockway, like Randolph, represents African Americans hidden from view in actual and symbolic basements. Ellison often highlights their invisible underground authority, their ambiguous situations both in relation to those actually in powerful positions and to their low social status. When Brockway describes his own life, he speaks volumes for and about others. He speaks for African Americans who work hidden in kitchens and fields and on assembly lines and for thousands of slaves buried underground. His description symbolizes the African American's paradoxical insider-outsider social position.[15]

As Brockway continues his conversation with Invisible Man, he says he has been making paint for twenty-five years. His pride is partly racial. He tells Invisible Man: *"We the machines inside the machines. . . . I know more about this basement than anybody. . . . I knows the location of each and every pipe and switch and cable and wire and everything else — both in the floors and in the walls and out in the yard. Yes sir! And what's more, I got it in my head so good I can trace it out on paper down to the last nut and bolt."* [16] Brockway presents himself as a founding presence within the company. He is the last word, the ultimate authority at Liberty Paints. It would be difficult to imagine the company without him. His presence at Liberty Paints is like that of African Americans in the United States. Since some slaves arrived before the *Mayflower*, African Americans have been around "ever since there's been a here."

After an explosion in the factory basement (perhaps set off by Brockway after he and Invisible Man come to blows), Invisible Man lands in the hospital. His hospitalization and recovery are often read by critics as symbolic episodes of death and rebirth. Thereafter, Invisible Man becomes intensely concerned about his identity. One day he stumbles upon the eviction of an old black couple from their Harlem apartment by a white marshal and two other men. Something has changed Invisible Man since his fight with Lucius Brockway. He feels immediate empathy toward the old couple when he sees their belongings thrown unceremoniously on the sidewalk: "And in a basket I saw a straightening comb, switches of false hair, a curling iron, a card with silvery letters against a background of dark red velvet, reading 'God Bless Our Home'; . . . I saw . . . a small Ethiopian flag, a faded tintype of Abraham Lincoln, and the smiling image of a Hollywood movie star torn from a magazine . . . an ornate greeting card with the message 'Grandma, I love you' in a childish scrawl; . . .

a celluloid baseball scoring card . . . and a dusty lock of infant hair tied with a faded and crumpled blue ribbon. . . . In my hand I held three lapsed life insurance policies with perforated seals stamped 'Void'; a yellowing newspaper portrait of a huge black man with the caption: MARCUS GARVEY DEPORTED."[17]

Here Invisible Man is at least as much a participant as an observer. Deeply moved by the old woman's sobbing, he stands in for a younger generation, the child who once scrawled "Grandma, I love you." He participates as though he is a close relative. But he is also like an anthropologist at a coveted American site, puzzling out the story of a family, a race, and a culture through objects and artifacts left behind. The straightening comb and curling irons definitively mark the couple as African American, representing many African American women who style their hair with these objects. The card proclaiming "God Bless Our Home," along with the family's Bible the old woman fights to get out of the marshal's hands, tell us that the old couple are Christians. "God Bless Our Home" is loaded with meaning; "Our Home" is America.

The couple's coveted keepsakes ironically show the discrepancies between their cherished ideals and brutal reality. The faded tintype of Abraham Lincoln, along with the image of the Hollywood star, evoke American mythology and call to the fore distinctions between fantasy and fact. The Ethiopian flag and the yellowing portrait of Marcus Garvey suggest that the couple may have been members of Garvey's United Negro Improvement Association. Garvey, a mythological figure too, symbolizes an ill-fated back-to-Africa movement. The images of Lincoln, who briefly supported colonization and deportation of slaves to Africa during the nineteenth century, and Garvey, who dramatizes that same possibility among black Harlemites during the 1920s, remind us of telling facts of African American history.[18]

The "Hollywood star torn from a magazine," perhaps *Life*, and the other Americana — photographs, images, mementos — form a revelatory gestalt of the moment: black Americans and white Americans, Hollywood and New York, Missouri reflected in "a commemorative plate celebrating the St. Louis World's Fair." The eviction of black octogenarians is, on one level, Dreiserian naturalism — a nasty and brutish slice of American life. On another, the contradictions of a nebulous past symbolized by the Ethiopian flag and the faded image of Abraham Lincoln remain alive. Furthermore, the evicted couple personify slavery and its consequences. Like Hawthorne's narrator discovering the embroidered scarlet "A" in the custom house and feeling its power, Invisible Man finds a relic with its own mystic vibrations: "My fingers closed upon something resting in a frozen footstep: a fragile paper, coming apart with age, written in black ink grown yellow. I read: FREE PAPERS. Be it known to all men that my negro, Primus Provo, has been freed by me this sixth day of August, 1859. *Signed*: John Samuels. Macon."[19]

The quaint legalese, the succinct rhetoric of manumission, still resonate with patriarchal authority — *my negro*. With palpable evidence in hand of his own direct link to slavery, Invisible Man experiences a shock of recognition, and he trembles. *Invisible Man* as talking book opens again. The free papers speak in an eloquent way to the very roots of African American literature, to slave narratives like Harriet Jacobs's *Incidents in the Life of a Slave Girl* and Frederick Douglass's *My Bondage and My Freedom*. Douglass and Jacobs document the displacements and disruptions of slavery and celebrate the cherished acquisition of their freedom. The free papers — releasing Primus Provo on August 6, 1859, in Macon, Georgia — focus Invisible Man's attention, forcing him to reflect upon the links between present and past, freedom and slavery: "I turned and stared at the jumble, no longer looking at what was before my eyes, but inwardly-outwardly, around a corner into the dark, far-away-and-long-ago, not so much of my own memory as of remembered words, of linked verbal echoes, images heard even when not listening at home. And it was as though I myself was being dispossessed of some painful yet precious thing which I could not bear to lose."[20] His own life is reconstructed through the lives of imaginary forebears. The jumble of objects becomes clear. Invisible Man is moved spontaneously to speak to the gathering crowd of black onlookers. He stokes their anger: "Look at them, they look like my mama and my papa and my grandma and grandpa, and I look like you and you look like me."[21]

Invisible Man does not yet understand the source of his own eloquence. But he has given us clues. His angry speech, issuing forth seemingly out of nowhere, represents the mental and emotional distillation of "remembered words, of linked verbal echoes, images heard even when not listening at home." He is compelled to speak for all. Struggling to puzzle out his encounters with his grandfather, Bledsoe, Mr. Norton, Trueblood, Brockway, Mary Rambo, and now

Primus Provo, Invisible Man becomes preoccupied with his own identity.

His self-searching eventually leads him to the Brotherhood — a communistic organization run by Brother Jack, its one-eyed white leader. Brother Jack persuades Invisible Man to join the Brotherhood, and he is shown around Brotherhood headquarters by Brother Tarp, an elderly, white-haired black man, reminiscent of Invisible Man's grandfather. Brother Tarp places a portrait of Frederick Douglass in Invisible Man's Brotherhood office. Invisible Man has heard of Douglass but has never consciously thought of Douglass in relation to himself: "For now I had begun to believe, . . . that there was a magic in spoken words. Sometimes I sat watching the watery play of light upon Douglass' portrait, thinking how magical it was that he had talked his way from slavery to government ministry. . . . What had his true name been? Whatever it was, it was as *Douglass* that he became himself, defined himself."[22] Douglass's portrait connects the novel to the history and consequences of slavery.

In the novel's concluding chapters, history, like Douglass's portrait, looms large. Invisible Man has an epiphany as he meditates on his personal life and the history of African Americans. His meditation on history is inspired by the death of Tod Clifton, a fellow black member of the Brotherhood, who is shot to death in Harlem by a white policeman. While leaving the scene of Clifton's death, Invisible Man observes several black boys standing on a Harlem subway platform. He looks at their clothes and listens to them talk. "The boys speak a jived-up transitional language full of country glamour, . . . think transitional thoughts though they dream the same old ancient dreams."[23] Then Invisible Man experiences a shock of recognition: "Now, moving through the crowds along 125th street, I was painfully aware of other men dressed like the boys, and of girls in dark exotic-colored stockings, their costumes surreal variations of downtown styles. They'd been there all along, but somehow I'd missed them. . . . They were outside the groove of history, and it was my job to get them in, all of them. . . . I moved with the crowd, . . . listening to the growing sound of a record shop loudspeaker blaring a languid blues. . . . Was this the only true history of the times, a mood blared by trumpets, trombones, saxophones and drums, a song with turgid inadequate words?"[24]

Invisible Man searches for language to express adequately the essential meaning of the moment captured by the sound of the brass horns — sounds that would quickly lose their meaning in the Harlem wind. He yearns for a more permanent historical record, one that would make visible and articulate the lives defined by transitional language and country glamour. Ellison's own sense of historical complexity comes through. Harlem was perhaps "Nowhere," as Harlemites used to say, except that it just happened to be in the world's greatest twentieth-century city. Furthermore, long before World War II, Harlem had its own rich and ethnically diverse history.

In "The Black Writer's Use of Memory," Melvin Dixon reflects upon Harlem's demographics from the area's beginnings to the 1990s; "A short walk in the vicinity brings you in contact with black people of every shade and texture . . . living on streets that have changed their names to Frederick Douglass Boulevard, . . . Marcus Garvey Park, and Adam Clayton Powell Boulevard. . . . This exercise and reification of cultural memory reconstructs a history of that region that never included blacks until 1915. Harlem was not settled originally by blacks, nor was the great, spacious design of urban boulevards and vintage architecture designed for blacks, but for a wealthy white Euro-American population." [25] But it is unlikely that such a transition of Harlem's physical and figurative landscape would have happened without riots exploding in the streets and a similar revolution in the collective consciousness of Harlemites.

Harlem Riot: Jazz Aesthetics

In the novel's concluding chapter, a riot breaks out, recalling the actual Harlem race riot of the summer of 1943. [26] Ellison makes the event a focal point of his novel by placing it in the final chapter. Few critics have done aesthetic justice to this particular moment of creativity. Since the chapter is followed only by the narrator's reflective comments in the epilogue, one can read the riot as the explosive conclusion or climax to the story — one final instance of Invisible Man's coming to terms with American reality. Invisible Man speaks of "a night of chaos." Recall that Ellison, in his discussion of the singer Jimmy Rushing, asserts that the true jazz artist must find ways "to reduce the chaos of living to form." So Ellison's jazz artistry in the final chapter should be appreciated as a splendid extravaganza in which a series of surrealistic images unfold against a background of street sounds — gunshots, sirens, human voices, and an abundance of laughter. The sounds and images — interspersed with Invisible Man's conversations, interior monologues, flashbacks and dreams — form a gestalt of the ongoing riot.

Although Ellison may not have had either Ellington's music or Bearden's paintings consciously in mind while writing this final chapter, it will be useful to think analogously here. He was striving to achieve something different and something more than a realistic or documentary sense of the riot. In that light, Ellison's manipulation of sound recalls Ellington's, and his exaggerated imagery recalls Bearden's. Ellison, like the Duke, uses street sounds in an improvisational manner. As buildings burn and looters desperately run, one periodically hears the siren sounds of fire engines and gunshots. Such sounds, among numerous others, surface periodically like train whistles and horns in Ellington's work. Ellison has said explicitly that he never tried to copy Bearden. But he and Bearden shared basic artistic assumptions. Each artist tried to reveal the complexity of African Americans and to use as many artistic resources as possible to achieve that end. Although Ellison actually saw the riot taking place, the idea of presenting a Harlem riot scene merely as a grim spectacle of anger was unattractive to Ellison, the artist.

Ellison's imagery appears to anticipate some of Bearden's complex works like The Block (1971), a large collage of cut and pasted paper images and paint. In its six panels a series of Harlem scenes unfolds. One sees a barber shop, a liquor store, and a storefront church. A funeral is taking place. There is an Annunciation scene. Bearden paints the interiors of some of the brownstones, revealing the private lives of the tenants. Several couples, for instance, are making love. Writing of Bearden's depiction of Harlem, Ellison concludes: "Where any number of painters have tried to project the 'prose' of Harlem, . . . Bearden has concentrated upon releasing its poetry, abiding rituals and ceremonies of affirmation, creating a surreal poetry compounded of vitality and powerlessness, destructive impulse and the all-pervading and enduring faith in their own style of American humanity. . . . His combination of technique is in itself eloquent of the sharp breaks, leaps in consciousness, distortions, paradoxes, reversals, telescoping of time and surreal blendings of styles, values, hopes and dreams which characterize much of Negro American history." [27]

Because of Ellison's dedication, like Bearden's, to portraying "the marvelous and the terrible" in African American life, the writer parodies novelistic realism in a series of interlocking scenes or panels. He places unexpected images of the riot in the foreground, capturing its absurdity and humor as much as he does the explosive black rage that is its source. Near the beginning of the chapter, Invisible Man, a participant-observer in the riot, is almost run over by looters, including two men rolling a safe down the street. He witnesses "a woman moving slowly past with a row of about a dozen dressed chickens suspended by their necks from the handle of a new straw broom." [28] Then he describes another cartoonish scene: "I saw a little hard man come out of the crowd carrying several boxes. He wore three hats upon his head, and several pairs of suspenders flopped about his shoulders, and . . . he wore a pair of gleaming new rubber hip boots. His pockets bulged and . . . he carried a cloth sack that swung heavily behind him." [29]

The image of the woman with the chickens suspended on a broom followed by the man wearing three hats is a part of what Invisible Man describes as "the absurdity of the whole night." Buildings are burning and people are dying. A group of men, having persuaded Invisible Man to come along, are filling buckets with kerosene to burn down the dilapidated apartment building where some of them live with their families. But even as they prepare for their act of arson, they are distracted. Invisible Man says: "And I saw a crowd of men running up pulling a Borden's milk wagon, on top of which, surrounded by a row of railroad flares, a huge woman in a gingham pinafore sat drinking beer from a barrel which sat before her. The men would run furiously a few paces and stop, resting between the shafts . . . shouting and laughing and drinking from a jug, as she on top threw back her head and shouted passionately in a full-throated voice of blues singer's timbre: 'If it hadn't been for the referee, / Joe Louis woulda killed / Jim Jefferie / Free beer!! . . .' Then she laughed and drank deeply while reaching over nonchalantly with her free hand to send quart after quart of milk crashing into the street. . . . Around me there were shouts of laughter and disapproval." [30]

Police officers in helmets, carrying or firing their pistols, some riding on horseback, are present in almost every scene. Shortly after Invisible Man sees the woman on top of the milk wagon, he describes mounted policemen chasing looters: "I could see a crowd rushing a store that faced the intersection, moving in, and a fusillade of canned goods, salami, liverwurst, hogs heads and chitterlings belching out to those outside and a bag of flour bursting white upon them; as now out of the dark of the intersecting street two mounted policemen came at a gallop, heaving huge and heavy-hooved, charging straight into the swarming mass."[31] Ellison has vivid images throughout the novel, but his presentation of a swift series of absurd scenes serves as an aesthetic searchlight, emphasizing dimensions of the riot beyond anger and protest.

The encounter, for instance, between Invisible Man and Ras the Exhorter is a vivid example of this. Ras, a representative of militant black nationalism, calls upon the Harlemites to quit "the stupid looting." He urges them to join him and "burst in the armory and get guns and ammunition." He and his supporters view Invisible Man as a "lying traitor" to the black race, given his involvement in the Brotherhood. They intend to lynch him: "They moved in a tight-knit order, carrying sticks and clubs, shotguns and rifles, led by Ras the Exhorter become Ras the Destroyer upon a great black horse. A new Ras of haughty, vulgar dignity, dressed in the costume of an Abyssinian chieftain; a fur cap upon his head, his arm bearing a shield, a cape made of the skin of some wild animal around his shoulder. A figure more out of a dream than out of Harlem, than out of even this Harlem night, yet real, alive, alarming."[32] Even in this "alarming" moment, Invisible Man views Ras as a figure "out of a dream."

As Invisible Man faces Ras and his angry followers, Ellison turns the novel away from the riot and its consequences to philosophical questions concerning individual identity. He returns to his sustained meditation on invisibility:

> I looked at Ras on his horse and at their handful of guns and rec-
> ognized the absurdity of the whole night and of the simple yet con-
> foundingly complex arrangement of hope and desire, fear and
> hate, that had brought me here still running, and knowing now
> who I was and where I was and knowing too that I had no longer
> to run for or from the Jacks and Emersons and the Bledsoes and
> Nortons, but only from their confusion, impatience and refusal to
> recognize the beautiful absurdity of their American identity and
> mine. I stood there, knowing that by dying, that being hanged by
> Ras on this street in this destructive night I would perhaps move

them one step closer to a definition of who they were and what I was and had been. But the definition would have been too narrow; I was invisible and hanging would not bring me to visibility, even to their eyes. . . . And I knew that it was better to live out one's own absurdity than to die for that of others, whether for Ras's or Jack's.[33]

Invisible Man mentions "absurdity" in three different contexts. He recognizes "the absurdity of the whole night." Then, as though speaking for Ellison himself, he refers to "the beautiful absurdity of their American identity and mine." And in the end he speaks of "living out one's own absurdity." Shortly thereafter, Invisible Man grabs Ras's spear and throws it back at him — stabbing him through the cheek. He runs desperately away from a mob of Ras's supporters and falls into an uncovered manhole. He finds himself — the manhole cover having been replaced by policemen — lighting the contents of his briefcase: his high-school diploma, Tod Clifton's dancing doll, the slip of paper spelling out his Brotherhood name.

The scene of incineration has often been discussed as Ellison's own symbolic finale — the validating personal effects of his youth and past are consumed by flames. The resulting light allows Invisible Man to find his way to a coal cellar. He resigns himself to a state of hibernation and contemplation. However, he becomes angry and for days throws himself about in self-destructive rage. He collapses, remaining in "a state neither of dreaming or waking, but somewhere in between."[34]

Invisible Man's final chapter is definitively Ellisonian. Albert Murray's comments, which deftly characterize the genius of Ellington and Picasso, come to mind. Murray concluded: "Whatever Ellington played became Ellington, and whatever Picasso painted became a Picasso." Ellison leaves us with a portentous dream, which, given its placement, provides a dramatic synthesis of his major chords. The chapter is a prose rendition of extravagant chord progressions or "changes" and dramatic recapitulation. Like a trumpeter playing chorus after chorus of "Blue Skies" or "Trumpet No End," Ellison takes us on a solo flight of familiar themes — now muted, distorted, and glissed — but nevertheless recognizable. His synthesis partly involves a continuation of his exaggerated use of imagery. Indeed, some of the images in the final scenes, given their surrealistic drama and mystery, seem closer to Salvador Dali than to Bearden. They clearly show Ellison's inspired creativity.

At the beginning of Invisible Man's dream, Ellison arranges a curtain call of principal characters: "I lay the prisoner of a group consisting of Jack and old Emerson and Bledsoe and Norton and Ras and the school superintendent and a number of others whom I failed to recognize." [35] Invisible Man says later: "All their faces were so vivid that they seemed to stand before me beneath a spotlight." [36] Like the powerful white men who taunted and laughed during his speech after the battle royal in the novel's opening chapter, Jack and the others laugh and grill him sarcastically. They angrily demand that Invisible Man "return to them." He refuses, and they castrate him:

> But now they came forward with a knife, holding me; and I felt the bright red pain and they took the two bloody blobs and cast them over the bridge, and out of my anguish I saw them curve up and catch beneath the apex of the curving arch of the bridge, to hang there, dripping down through the sunlight into the dark red water. And while the others laughed, before my pain-sharpened eyes the whole world was slowly turning red. [37]

Since the riot takes place in Harlem, perhaps we are to imagine the bridge to be the George Washington. That would partly explain the symbolic and surreal image of his "seed" and blood "dripping down through the sunlight."

Here it will be useful to remember Ellison's praise of Bearden. He applauds Bearden for revealing "the mysterious complexity of those who dwell in our urban slums," but concludes that Bearden's "is the eye of the painter, not that of a sociologist." Similarly, we see in Ellison's arrangement and orchestration of images, themes, characters, and scenes a revelation of the mysterious complexity of his own aesthetic originality. For while the scene described above recapitulates the brutal violence, and echoes the wicked laughter, of those whites who witnessed lynchings and castrations of black men, slave and free, one can hardly mistake Ellison's rendition of the subject for that of a sociologist, a historian, or even a militant black aesthetician.

Invisible Man, though castrated, laughs in his tormentors' faces. They want to know why, and he gives them a metaphysical reply: "That there hang not only my generations wasting upon the water. . . ." They insist that he go on. He adds: "There's your universe, and that drip-drop upon the water you hear is all the history you've made, all you're going to make. Now laugh, you scientists. Let's hear you laugh."[38] This scene, the "drip-drop" of Invisible Man's "seed" upon the water; his reference to "generations," "universe," and "history" reveal Ellisonian assumptions about the fundamental workings of American culture. His major chords — unity, ambiguity, discipline, possibility, and transcendence — are all suggested here. Invisible Man's comments suggest an inexorable historical connection — a unity — between his life and the lives of his tormentors. Theirs is a tragicomic relationship, one of ambiguity lacking any obvious connection. A stern discipline will clearly be needed if particular individuals, let alone the nation, are to rise to the occasion to transcend various obstacles and make real the possibility of democracy.

Invisible Man's comments also recall earlier points in the novel. They take us back to statements Mr. Norton made at the Golden Day. Mr. Norton, a trustee at Invisible Man's former college, has fainted. Invisible Man, his guide and chauffeur, takes him to the Golden Day, a local watering hole and brothel for disturbed veterans. While there, Norton encounters one vet who is a wise fool. When the vet asks Norton why he has been interested in the school, Norton answers, "Out of a sense of my destined role. . . . I felt, and still feel, that your people are in some important way tied to my destiny."[39] The scene also reminds us of Lucius Brockway and Liberty Paints. Drops of "black dope" are a crucial ingredient for the production of "optic white," the company's best white paint. And Lucius Brockway, the old black worker deep in the basement, tells Invisible Man: "Everybody knows I been here ever since there's been a here — even helped dig the first foundation."[40]

Moreover, Invisible Man's assertions about history and generations are characteristic of a theme that Ellison would return to in *Juneteenth*. There, Rev. A. Z. Hickman, a principal character, delivers a long sermon in which he refers to the planting of "seed" and the redemptive rebirth of dismembered black bodies out of American soil. In Ellison's transcendent view of the inextricable nature of African American and American reality — the unity in the diversity of American life—even the death of African Americans, whether by lynching or gunshots, may ultimately lead to redemption. This phenomenon is what Invisible Man has in mind when, referring to Jack and the others, he speaks of "the beautiful absurdity of their American identity and mine."

We have seen how throughout his final chapter Ellison focuses on absurdity in various ways. We are left to ponder the riddle suggested in the final fantastic image. In Invisible Man's dream the bridge rises from its position: "And high above me now the bridge seemed to move off to where I could not see, striding like a robot, an iron man, whose iron legs clanged doomfully as it moved. And then I struggled up, full of sorrow and pain, shouting, 'No, no, we must stop him.'"[41] Perhaps the bridge-turned-iron-man is the bridge that connects the present to the past and the future, a necessary connection for the accurate perception of "the beautiful absurdity" of American identity. Indeed, Invisible Man worries as he awakens from the dream or nightmare that his tormentors are still "all up there somewhere, making a mess of the world."[42]

Throughout his final chapter, Ellison's orchestration of the images and scenes that Invisible Man views also involves the protagonist's own searching introspection. Furthermore, in the epilogue Invisible Man's explicit motivation for writing mirrors Ellison's:

> So why do I write, torturing myself to put it down? . . . Why should I be the one to dream this nightmare? Why should I be dedicated and set aside — yes, if not to at least tell a few people about it? . . . So it is that now I denounce and defend. . . . I condemn and affirm, say no and say yes, say yes and say no. I denounce because though implicated and partially responsible, I have been hurt to the point of abysmal pain, hurt to the point of invisibility. And I defend because in spite of all I find that I love. In order to get some of it down I have to love. . . . So I denounce and I defend and I hate and I love.[43]

Here we should note two crucial points. Ellison the novelist, it was proposed earlier, is a metaphysical rebel. This characterization constitutes a deliberate attempt to remove Ellison from all forms of ideological categorization — whether integrationist, nationalist, or elitist. The phrase is essentially a description of his aesthetic stance. The preceding passage, for instance, concerns the torture necessarily involved in wrestling with the angel Art. The true artist must remain open to all perspectives and emotions: "I condemn and affirm, say no and say yes, say yes and say no. . . . I denounce and I defend and I hate and I love." Avoiding a political characterization of Ellison the artist is particularly appropriate in a concluding chapter focusing on a riot. Guessing, for example, at whether the novelist approves or disapproves of the riot is not especially useful. Yet it is appropriate to ask what purpose it serves in Ellison's aesthetic universe. What does "metaphysical rebel" mean in aesthetic terms?

At points in *Invisible Man* (and in sections of *Juneteenth*) Ellison the novelist emerges as a relatively subversive figure. As an artist, he seems dedicated more to the discovery and presentation of the absurdity of the riot than to its social causes or destructive consequences. Even when the discussion is ostensibly political, it is simultaneously challenged and undercut by the visual absurdity of various scenes. The philosophical forays of particular characters — whether Invisible Man or Lee Willie Minifees, the jazzman from one of the sections intended for *Juneteenth* who burns his white Cadillac on a senator's lawn — are Ellisonian bridges, or transitions, to further action.

Jazz in Progress
Juneteenth, Ellison's Second Novel

*I believe that true novels even when most pessimistic and bitter arise out of an
impulse to celebrate human life and therefore are ritualistic and ceremonial at their
core. Thus they would preserve as they destroy, affirm as they reject.*
— Ralph Ellison, "The World and the Jug"

The Long Wait: Ellison and Poetic Closure

In both the prologue and the epilogue of *Invisible Man*, Ellison's
nameless character makes statements that have turned out to be
prophetic about Ellison's own relationship to his second novel, *Juneteenth*. In the prologue, Invisible Man says, "It is incorrect to assume
that, because I'm invisible and live in a hole, I am dead. I am neither
dead nor in a state of suspended animation. Call me Jack-the-Bear, for
I am in a state of hibernation."[1] He returns to the image of hibernation in the epilogue and describes the consequences of that liminal
state: "So I took to the cellar; I hibernated. I got away from it all. But
that wasn't enough. I couldn't be still even in hibernation. Because,
damn it, there was the mind, the mind. It wouldn't let me rest. Gin,
jazz and dreams were not enough. Books were not enough."[2] Like his
character, Ralph Ellison the novelist appeared to hibernate as the
world waited for forty-two years — from the publication of *Invisible
Man* in 1952 to the day of his death in 1994 — for his second novel. Although he published eight sections of it (from the 1950s through the
1970s), the novel did not appear during his lifetime.

Random House published *Juneteenth* in 1999.[3] However, in the
opening sentence of his review of the novel for the *New York Times Book
Review*, Louis Menand concluded: "This is not Ellison's second

novel." He sums up what is becoming the prevalent view of the first published version of Ellison's long-awaited book. In "Unfinished Business," Menand criticizes John Callahan, Ellison's literary executor and editor of the novel, for his failure to rise to the occasion of Ellison's noble literary intentions and the voluminous manuscript's jazz-like intensity and complicated developments.

Noting that the literary executor received no instructions from Ellison and pointing out that even the novel's title is Callahan's, Menand sums up Callahan's editorial process using information gleaned from Callahan's own afterword, "A Note to Scholars." Menand explains that the text of *Juneteenth* consists of a piece published in a literary magazine in 1960, the 1972 version of what Ellison called, in his notes, "Book 2," a thirty-eight-page manuscript called "Bliss's Birth," a paragraph from a piece entitled "Cadillac Flambé," and two passages from a "later version" of the manuscript. Pointing out that Callahan "made choices where Ellison was still meditating options," Menand provides a succinct catalogue of the editor's handiwork:

> Dr. Callahan performed the following surgery: he divided the text into 16 chapters (there are no chapter breaks in the original); arranged the episodes in "Book 2" in the sequence he thought most plausible (Ellison's drafts differed); tacked on the 1960 magazine piece as an opening chapter; patched the paragraph from "Cadillac Flambé" into what is now Chapter 2, which he also "slightly pruned"; excised "two brief passages" from Chapter 3; stuck the material from the "later version" of the manuscript into chapter 14 ("to intensify the action"); added the "Bliss's Birth" manuscript as Chapter 15; discarded "an intriguing but clearly unfinished" episode Ellison had intended as the final section and substituted a passage he thought "the most logical and emotional place to end" (evidently because it resonated with the paragraph from "Cadillac Flambé" he had inserted in Chapter 2); and wrote an introduction explaining what the novel is about.[4]

Despite Menand's negative assessment of Callahan's editorial process and the end result, it is important to understand the daunting challenge any editor would have faced. After a forty-odd-year gestation period, Callahan was forced to perform an unprecedented literary cesarean operation. Callahan says he examined "reams of manuscripts, dating back more than 20 years, plus 51 computer disks, most with episodes of the novel on them." He also took into account the published excerpts and Ellison's "scribblings on hundreds of scraps of paper" to puzzle out the precise sequences and the appropriate versions of the novel's numerous episodes. Ellison kept such drafts, Callahan says, "in almost endless, maddening variation."[5]

While Ellison did not leave instructions concerning the novel's completion, he did discuss its genesis and development. He told John Hersey in 1974: "I guess it started with the idea of an old man being so outraged with his life that he goes poking around in the cellar to find a forgotten coffin, which he had bought years before as insurance against his possible ruin. He discovers that he has lived so long that the coffin is full of termites, and that even the things he has stored in the coffin have fallen apart. . . . But then it led to another idea, which I wrote first, of a little boy being placed in a coffin in a ritual of death and transcendence, celebrated by a Negro evangelist who was unsure whether he was exploiting the circus-sideshow shock set off by a child rising up out of a coffin, or had hit upon an inspired way of presenting the sacred drama of the resurrection. In my mind all of this is tied up with being a Negro in America."[6]

Juneteenth (the published novel, not Ellison's previously published story of the same name) has a simple plot with a series of complex subplots. A young black boy named Bliss is light enough to pass for white. He is the sideman of Rev. Hickman, a jazz trombonist turned traveling preacher; young Bliss's job is to rise up on cue out of a coffin, wearing a white suit with tails. The kid hates the darkness of the coffin, but he has his favorite toys and a Bible to keep him company. One day in the middle of one of Hickman's sermons a red-haired white woman arrives (in the segregated South), declares that Bliss is her son, turns the coffin over, spilling out its contents—the toys, the Bible—and grabs Bliss. The black sisters of the church rush forward, pulling and tussling Bliss away. This existential struggle traumatizes him.

Several years later Bliss sneaks into a theatre for whites only, staying for hours. Rev. Hickman and the church members look for him, and eventually Hickman sees him coming out of the theatre. A year or two later Bliss disappears altogether. No one hears from him again until, after several decades, there is an assassination attempt (in the Senate chamber) on the racist Senator Sunraider. Bliss has become the senator.

A Jazzman Burns His White Cadillac

It is hardly an accident that Bliss's surrogate father — Hickman — is a trombone player turned preacher. Ellison's ongoing concern with the improvisational jazz-shape of American culture surfaces in his second novel. How could he write about what Ellington captures so deftly in "It Don't Mean a Thing If It Ain't Got That Swing," or what Bearden represents in works like *Wrapping It Up at the Lafayette* or *Uptown Sunday Night Session* or *The Block*? In one episode that was essentially excluded (Callahan includes one paragraph) from Random House's *Juneteenth*, Ellison displays his American vision and signature virtuosity. A version of the story was published in February 1973 in *American Review* as "Cadillac Flambé," the story of an angry black jazzman dressed in a white suit who makes a speech (unaware of the senator's hidden racial past), as he burns his white Cadillac on Senator Sunraider's manicured lawn.[7]

Ellison knew that this tale, flaming Cadillac and all, would capture the attention of American readers and critics who had been waiting since the 1950s for it. The bizarre ritual, the public burning of an automobile on the estate of a senator, was an arresting spectacle. The burning was the response of Lee Willie Minifees, the jazzman, to the senator who had referred to the Cadillac as a "coon cage." The scene, in the words of the white reporter-narrator McIntyre, is an American "*tableau vivant*" — a white Cadillac convertible destroyed by "leaping red and blue flames." The smell of alcohol and gasoline — what McIntyre (a "liberal ex-radical Northerner"), calls "those defining spirits of our age" — fills the air. The white convertible soon takes on an expressive life of its own. The flaming automobile appears to undergo metamorphosis, crying out in protest — through its short-circuited horn — against its fiery destruction.

To be sure, "Cadillac Flambé" is a self-contained vignette, one of many carefully crafted episodes in the original manuscript. And although Callahan chose to leave "Cadillac Flambé" out of *Juneteenth*, it dramatically emphasizes Ellison's ongoing belief in both the power and process of jazz as an art form and as a metaphor for the drama of democracy. McIntyre calls Minifees's interaction with the Cadillac a "duet."[8] It gives Lee Willie Minifees, the jazzman turned arsonist, the stage for his performance, his philosophical diatribe, his "duet" and solo. McIntyre is forced into the role of accompanist. Vamping, he must follow Minifees until the very end, when the siren sounds of the approaching police and firemen blend with the outcry of the Cadillac's horn.

As Robert O'Meally says, "A jazz piece usually has no rigidly set number of sections: the vamp may continue until it is virtually a piece unto itself; the choruses, solo breaks, and out-choruses may repeat until the bandleader, on a given night, calls a halt which can come quite suddenly and, for that matter, may meld easily into the piece which comes after it, as if an entire evening's performance was one extended skyscraper with a variety of stories and styles blended into one."[9]

In the light of O'Meally's description, "Cadillac Flambé" is a representative jazz episode, in which Ellison places his jazzman-arsonist at center stage. Jazz, like the skyscraper, is definitively American. So it is appropriate, given the writer's aesthetics, that Lee Willie Minifees, a bass player, is the mouthpiece for much of the narration. Ellison's orchestration of American images, objects, and scenes highlights his own jazzlike performance, a dramatic instance of his virtuosity and vision on display. If the writer's initial clues — Washington, D.C., as the setting, a U.S. senator, a white Cadillac, and "leaping red and blue flames" — do not readily suggest his orchestration of a patriotic ritual of sorts, he drives the point home by having the burning occur on Sunday. And McIntyre's words and phrases — "photographic rite of spring," "somber iconography," "religious symbolism," "sacrificial act," "spirit's materialization," "confession," "ecstatic chant," and "portentous political gesture" — strongly suggest a ritualistic ceremony. McIntyre ultimately concludes that Lee Willie Minifees's burning of his own car on the senator's lawn was "so extreme a reply as to be almost metaphysical."[10]

McIntyre, with tape recorder (to record bird songs) and binoculars in hand, is returning from a successful birdwatching expedition and a pleasant brunch when Minifees, driving unexpectedly across Senator Sunraider's lawn, stops him in his tracks. McIntyre views himself as the most objective of journalists, but, as with Melville's Captain Delano, his blind spots are as revelatory as his insights. He describes the "majestic roar" of Senator Sunraider that incited Minifees to destroy his white Cadillac. And with tape recorder in hand, he captures the jazzman's "typically Negro" voice. Using McIntyre as narrator-reporter, Ellison extravagantly offers three points of view — McIntyre's, Senator Sunraider's, and Lee Willie Minifees's — three different, though distinctly American, voices. Furthermore, McIntyre records a "duet," the "swoosh-pop-crackle-and hiss" of the flaming Cadillac as the jazzman yells, chants, and even sings for the stunned onlookers.

McIntyre is congenial and charming, and knows how to turn a nice phrase. After his birdwatching and brunch, he reports: "And after the beef bouillon ran out, our host, an ingenious man, improvised a drink from chicken broth and vodka which he proclaimed the 'chicken-shot.' This was all very pleasant and after a few drinks my spirits were soaring. . . . I had paused to notice how the Senator's lawn rises from the street with a gradual and imperceptible elevation that makes the mansion, set far at the top, seem to float like a dream castle; an illusion intensified by the chicken-shots." [11]

Looking through his binoculars, McIntyre sees the senator "dressed in chef's cap, apron and huge asbestos gloves." Senator Sunraider is preparing a barbecue and entertaining his "notable guests" by "displaying his great talent for mimicking his colleagues." McIntyre views Senator Sunraider as an entertainer, something of an actor-ventriloquist, expertly acting out the personalities of others and revealing something of his own. Aided by the chicken-shots, McIntyre sees the senator's estate as a "dream castle."

The dream is shattered when he sees Minifees driving his Cadillac across the senator's lawn. The black jazzman waves to the gathering crowd as he gets out, and McIntyre sizes him up: "The top was back and the driver, smiling as though in a parade, was a well-dressed Negro man of about thirty-five, who sported the gleaming hair affected by their jazz musicians and prizefighters. . . . The waving I interpreted as the expression of simple-minded high spirits aroused by the driver's pleasure in piloting such a luxurious automobile, the simple exuberance of a Negro allowed a role in what he considered an important public spectacle." [12]

McIntyre focuses on Minifees's dramatic sense of occasion and the jazzman's stylized driving show — in McIntyre's words, "his ceremonial attention to form." McIntyre is calling attention to what Ellison views as African American elegance. In an interview Ellison gave in 1976, he remarked: "Elegance turns up in every aspect of Afro-American culture, from sermons to struts, pimp-walks, and dance steps. . . . And doesn't all that Afro-American adoration of the Cadillac speak of elegance? Look at the elegance with which the dedicated worshipper of the Cadillac sits at the steering wheel of his chariot." [13]

To McIntyre, Minifees's Cadillac is a "shining chariot." But McIntyre is hardly concerned about elegance in the sense that Ellison uses it. He is merely doing his reporter's job by capturing the mood of a performance. When he describes the jazzman's "gleaming hair," his "objective" description betrays his own deep-seated prejudice — "the gleaming hair affected by their [my emphasis] jazz musicians and prize fighters." By "their" McIntyre clearly means "Negroes," thereby excluding himself, as a white American reporter, from "their" world. This is a characteristic instance of Ellisonian irony. The American scene unfolding before McIntyre's eyes necessarily includes him. The story takes place during the 1950s, when jazz musicians and prize fighters like Louis Armstrong, Duke Ellington, Nat King Cole, Sugar Ray Robinson, and Floyd Patterson were household names. Given their talent and achievement, let alone their tonsorial flair and colorful manners of self-presentation, they were highly influential in American culture.

McIntyre's attribution of a definitive otherness to black jazz musicians and prize fighters, and by extension all Negroes, is amplified by his description of Minifees's "simple-minded high spirits" and "the simple exuberance of a Negro." In contrast, Minifees's own sense of himself is the exact opposite. Everything about him — his white Cadillac, his gleaming hair, his jazz music, and his unexpected reply to the senator — constitute a studied display of self-pride and racial vanity, an embodiment of his own style and considered point of view.

The reporter's lapse into cultural subjectivity does not ruin his story. After Minifees takes his bull fiddle and bow out of the car along with a wooden knitting needle and tennis ball, the journalist reports, "a certain tension as during the start of a concert" was building up. Minifees's instrument, the bull fiddle, is another symbolic clue. The jazz critic Stanley Crouch writes: "In jazz, the bass is protean in its identity and function. That jazz bass is percussive, harmonic, and lyric. It is the Southern end of the music, the bottom, the lower frequency. Known as the bull fiddle, its player is sometimes a matador whose imagination is a syncopating cape turning the snorting power of that wood and those four thick strings this way and that."[14]

The tempo accelerates when Lee Willie Minifees connects the tennis ball to the knitting needle, ignites it and shoots his "improvised [emphasis mine] flamed-tipped arrow onto the cloth top of the convertible." A woman in the crowd yells, "Why that black son of the devil!" The bizarre "concert" is about to begin. McIntyre, now an accompanist of sorts, speeds up the tempo of his sentences: "I had the impression of a wall of heat springing from the grass before me. Then the flames erupted with a stunning blue roar that sent the spectators scattering. People were shouting now and through the blue flames before me I could see the Senator and his guests running from the terrace to halt at the top of the lawn, looking down, while behind me there were screams, the grinding of brakes, the thunder of footfalls as the promenaders broke in a great spontaneous wave up the grassy slope, then sensing the danger of exploding gasoline, receded hurriedly to a safer distance below, their screams and curses ringing above the roar of flames." [15]

McIntyre, one of the "unwilling participants" in the "primitive ceremony," has been forced by his professional training to rise to the occasion and get the story. He describes a cacophony of sounds: screams, grinding brakes, footfalls, curses, and the roar of flames. As the white Cadillac burns, he describes what he sees through the blue flames with his own rhythmic string of gerunds. He places or indeed plays his gerunds, like so many sharps and flats, at appropriate intervals. He records the mood by using "springing," "scattering," "shouting," "running," "looking," "grinding," "sensing," "exploding," "ringing," and "stunning." At moments his words rhyme — "springing," "ringing." [16]

The stage is set for Minifees's long and "improvised" speech, the sound and accents of his "strong and hoarse and typically Negro" voice. McIntyre struggles for the reporter's "dedicated objectivity," yet he remains at the mercy of his subjectivity. Like an accompanist heard for a few bars during a lengthy solo, he periodically makes brief statements or raises questions. His brief interventions help underscore Ellison's overall intent. On one level, Ellison is clearly celebrating (in the Whitmanian sense) the wonders of the United States — jazz, the automobile, improbable politicians, the improvised nature of American culture. He is dramatizing as well a distinctly American set of circumstances. The episode, like the novel as a whole, is a metaphysical parable about the complex fate of being American.

Like McIntyre, Minifees struggles in counterpoint for his own brand of objectivity. His speech is delivered as an odd expression of contrition. He politely urges his growing audience to calm down: "Ladies and gentlemen . . . please don't be disturbed! I don't mean you any harm, and if you'll just cool it a minute I'll tell you what this is all about." He explicitly suggests that his act of arson be read as a jazz performance when he calls the names of several jazz musicians he admires. As he was speeding from Chattanooga back to his home in Harlem, he heard Senator Sunraider's offensive speech on the radio: "I was just hoping to hear some Dinah [Washington] or Duke [Ellington] or Hawk [Coleman Hawkins] so that I could study their phrasing and improve my style and enjoy myself. — But what do I get? . . . I GOT THAT NO GOOD, NOWHERE SENATOR SUNRAIDER! THAT'S WHAT I GOT! AND WHAT WAS HE DOING? HE WAS TRYING TO GET THE UNITED STATES GOVERNMENT TO MESS WITH MY CADILLAC! AND WHAT'S MORE HE WAS CALLING MY CADDY A 'COON CAGE.'"[17]

Minifees warns the crowd that the senator was "playing the dozens" with his Cadillac, an allusion to a ritualistic game of insult and repartee practiced among many African Americans. He raises his volume and accents every note when he describes the senator. After all, Minifees has been studying the phrasing of "Hawk." Coleman Hawkins, a tenor saxophonist, was famous for his complicated style. By printing some of Minifees's comments in bold capital letters, a pattern he follows throughout the jazzman's performance, Ellison (via McIntyre) gives instructions on how to read Minifees's words. The jazzman blasts out, "NO GOOD NO WHERE SENATOR SUNRAIDER" in Negro fortissimo. At other points (and in plain text) the jazzman lowers the volume but picks up his tempo, taking us on an introspective solo flight — extemporaneously reconstructing and retelling the story of his decision to "sacrifice" his Cadillac.[18]

In the hands of a lesser artist, Minifees's long speech would seem merely another portentous diatribe or a caricature of an irate Negro cussing out a white man. But Ellison, like Twain, deftly captures an instance of African American "loud-talking" and the playing of the "dozens" — overlapping vernacular traditions defined by spontaneity, hyperbole, self-mockery, and humor. Minifees's speech is shot through with humorous asides and astute perceptions about the workings of American culture. The "capper" that decisively leads him to the senator's lawn is what he imagines the kids in Harlem will say: "Folks standing on the streets and hanging out of windows will sing out, 'HEY! THERE GOES MISTER COON AND HIS COON CAGE.' . . . And all those little husky-voiced colored CHILDREN playing in the gutters will point at you and say, 'THERE GOES MIS-TAH GOON AND HIS GOON GAGE' and that will be right in Harlem! . . . That was the capper, and THAT'S why I'm here!" [19]

A Jazzman's Duet and Solo

The crowd, no longer "asking puzzled questions," remains silent. The jazzman plays the dozens with the senator's assumptions, mocking him in a complicated pattern of loud accusatory shouts, momentary apologies, and professorial musings. He ends his long speech with an "ecstatic chant," punctuating his angry words by stamping his feet:

> Listen to me, Senator: I don't want no JET! (stamp!) But thank you kindly.
> I don't want no FORD! (stamp!)
> Neither do I want a RAMBLER! (stamp!)
> I don't want no NINETY-EIGHT! (stamp!)
> Ditto the THUNDERBIRD! (stamp-stamp!)
> Yes, and keep those CHEVYS and CHRYSLERS away from me — do you (stamp!) *hear* me, Senator?
> YOU HAVE TAKEN THE BEST . . . SO, DAMMIT, TAKE ALL THE REST! Take ALL the rest! . . .
> So to keep you happy, I, me, Lee Willie Minifees, am prepared to WALK. I'm ordering me some club-footed, pigeon-toed SPACE SHOES. I'd rather crawl or FLY. I'd rather save my money and wait until the A-RABS make a car. The Zulus even. Even the ES-KIMOS! Oh, I'll walk and wait. I'll grab me a GREYHOUND or a FREIGHT! SO you can have my coon cage, fare thee well! [20]

Minifees shouts: "YOU HAVE TAKEN THE BEST . . . SO, DAMMIT TAKE ALL THE REST." His words signal defiant resignation. Whatever the object or subject of the contest was before the words are uttered no longer matters. Minifees scores again when he says sarcastically to the astonished onlookers: "I am here, ladies and gentlemen, to present the Senator a present." Addressing Senator Sunraider directly, he adds: "I hope all of my people do likewise. Because after your speech they ought to run whenever they even look at one of these. They ought to make for the bomb shelters whenever one comes close to the curb." [21]

Ellison exploits Minifees's voice, which McIntyre describes as "typically Negro," as "black English." His ungrammatical string of double negatives — "I don't want no JET! . . . I don't want no FORD!" — seems wholly congruent with his mocking use of hyperbole. He is also "signifying" when he says sarcastically: "I'd rather save my money and wait until the A-rabs make a car." Ellison emphasizes a "typical" Negro pronunciation, indeed mispronunciation, of "Arabs" — often pronounced as two words "A-rabs," with the "A" heavily accented. His statement is intended to match the senator's insulting, if "majestic," roar.[22]

The jazzman comically suggests that he is prepared to purchase a foreign product, even one not yet invented. Ellison does not create such a colorful speaker for comic relief, but allows Minifees to put on marvelous display sources and tropes of American English. Minifees, a dedicated artist trying to improve his style, has, like Ellison, high artistic standards. He will settle for nothing less than the best.

At the end of the episode, McIntyre explains what Senator Sunraider said that sparked Minifees's eruption. The senator's comments, made in a committee session, had been televised and aired over the radio. McIntyre points out that they were "mild and far short of his usual maliciousness," but Senator Sunraider did not mince words: "We have reached a sad state of affairs, gentlemen, wherein this fine product of American skill and initiative has become so common in Harlem that much of its initial value has been sorely compromised. Indeed I am led to suggest, and quite seriously, that legislation be drawn up to rename it the 'Coon Cage Eight.' And not at all because of its eight, super-efficient cylinders, nor because of the lean, springing strength and beauty of its general outlines. Not at all, but because it has now become such a common sight to see eight or more of our darker brethren crowded together enjoying its power, its beauty, its neo-pagan comfort, while weaving recklessly through the streets of our great cities and our super-highways."[23]

It is Ellison's sense of American irony that has the black jazzman and the white Senator praise the Cadillac in similar patriotic terms as "the very best." Each focuses on its design and its new technological features. Minifees invites the senator to "ENJOY the automatic dimmer and the power brakes. ROLL, Mister Senator, with that fluid DRIVE. Breathe that air-conditioned AIR," while the Senator applauds its "eight super-efficient cylinders" and the "beauty of its general outlines." Their perspectives diverge only when the senator makes it clear that Cadillacs are not made for Harlemites: "Give your attention to who it is that is creating the scarcity and removing these superb machines from the reach of those for whom they were intended! With so many of these good things, what, pray, do those people desire — is it a jet plane on every Harlem rooftop?" [24]

Throughout the episode, the white Cadillac becomes increasingly expressive. At first, the "shining chariot" comes gleaming into view surrounded by its own aura of glamorous vitality. McIntyre admires its "rich ivory leather upholstery" and watches as the convertible top starts "rising from its place of concealment to soar into place like the wing of some great, slow, graceful bird." During Minifees's passionate confession of his love for his "scientific dreamboat," McIntyre refers to the jazzman's "duet with the expiring Cadillac." Minifees simultaneously defends "THE BEST" against "ALL THE REST" and against Senator Sunraider's "NASTY MOUTH." Minifees's "duet" continues as he unexpectedly starts singing "God Bless America." He implores the stunned onlookers to join in before he is arrested. As he hears the sound of approaching police sirens, he tells the crowd: "I want you to understand that that was a damned GOOD Caddy and I loved her DEARLY. That's why you don't have to worry about me. . . . Because, remember, nothing makes a man feel better than giving AWAY something, than SACRIFICING something that he dearly LOVES!" [25] Minifees's idiosyncratic expression of personal pride recalls Invisible Man's decision to live out his own absurdity rather than to die for that of others.

The Cadillac, with seeming anthropomorphic intelligence, appears to understand when it is needed to perform on cue. The "duet" ends as Minifees is about to be arrested and handcuffed. He continues singing along with "the doleful wailing of the car." The flaming Cadillac's short-circuited horn delivers a haunting swan song that blends with Minifees's voice and the siren sounds. The crowd becomes mourners, apparently "weeping" over the Cadillac's violent death. McIntyre reports: "Some continued to shout threats in their outrage and frustration, while others, both men and women, filled the air with a strangely brokenhearted and forlorn sound of weeping. . . . In fact, they continued to mill angrily about even as firemen in asbestos suits . . . sprayed the flaming car with a foamy chemical, which left it looking like the offspring of some strange animal." [26]

Ellison has crafted this episode as a national allegory. There are allusions to the Washington Monument, automobiles, baseball, football, radio, television, and air conditioning. Various states and cities appear throughout the episode — Washington, D.C., Chattanooga, Oklahoma, New York, and, of course, Harlem.

Readers of "Cadillac Flambé" did not know about Senator Sunraider's complex evolution from Bliss, the boy evangelist of dubious origins. Readers of Random House's *Juneteenth* still do not learn the identity, black or white, of Bliss's biological father. In *Juneteenth*, Bliss's white mother never tells even Hickman that powerful secret. However, it is clear that Bliss/Sunraider has used his rhetorical skills, honed at the knee of Rev. A. Z. Hickman, the former jazz trombonist, to put the "NASTY MOUTH" on blacks, the better to win the friendship and votes of prejudiced whites. The whole episode represents a peculiarly American brand of social absurdity, a national allegory disguised as a parodic episode.

Jazz Preaching
Reverend Hickman and the Battered Silver Trombone

I contend that the Negro is the creative voice of America, is creative America, and it was a happy day in America when the first unhappy slave was landed on its shores.

There, in our tortured induction into this "land of liberty," we built its most graceful civilization. Its wealth, its flowering fields and handsome homes; its pretty traditions; its guarded leisure and music, were all our creations.

We stirred in our shackles and our unrest awakened Justice in the hearts of a courageous few, and we recreated in America the desire for true democracy, freedom for all, the brotherhood of man, principles on which the country had been founded.

We were freed and as before, we fought America's wars, provided her labor, gave her music, kept alive her flickering conscience, prodded her on toward the yet unachieved goal, democracy — until we became more than a part of America! We — this kicking, yelling, touchy, sensitive, scrupulously demanding minority — are the personification of the ideal begun by the Pilgrims almost 350 years ago.

— Duke Ellington, in The Duke Ellington Reader, *edited by Mark Tucker*

The Performed Word

Lee Willie Minifees's burning of his white Cadillac convertible on the senator's lawn greatly disturbed the senator. The jazzman's white suit and his preacher's style of oration stirred deep-seated memories that the senator had long repressed. He himself, as a boy in Hickman's church, had worn a white suit with tails. It was his costume in set performances with the traveling evangelist known both as "Daddy Hickman" and "God's Trombone," a jazz trombonist turned preacher.

In *Juneteenth* Rev. Hickman delivers a commemorative oration partly based on "The Valley of the Dry Bones," or "Dry Bones in the Valley," a black folk sermon. In his preface to *God's Trombones: Seven Negro Sermons in Verse* (1927), James Weldon says he recalls hearing sermons passed "from preacher to preacher and from locality to locality."[1] One such sermon, "The Valley of the Dry Bones," retold the vision of the Old Testament prophet Ezekiel. His vision is a testament to God's mysterious and miraculous power. A valley of dry bones undergoes metamorphosis, rises up, and becomes an army of Christian soldiers.

> The hand of the Lord was upon me, and carried me out in the spirit of the Lord, and set me down in the midst of the valley which was full of bones, and caused me to pass by them round about: and, behold, there were very many in the open valley; and, lo, they were very dry. And he said unto me, Son of man, can these bones live? . . . So I prophesied as I was commanded: and as I prophesied, there was a noise, and behold a shaking, and the bones came together, bone to his bone. And when I beheld, lo, the sinews and the flesh came up upon them, and the skin covered them. . . . And the breath came into them, and they lived, and stood up upon their feet, an exceeding great army. (Ezekiel 37: 1–4, 7–10)

Johnson describes the charismatic power of the "old-time" Negro preacher. Although few of them were formally educated, some possessed "positive genius." He concludes: "The earliest of these preachers must have virtually committed many parts of the Bible to memory through hearing the scriptures read or preached from in the white churches which the slaves attended." Johnson describes their "secret of oratory, . . . a progression of rhythmic words." He had "witnessed congregations moved to ecstasy by the rhythmic intoning of sheer incoherences." The preacher's voice was often "a marvelous instrument, a voice he could modulate from a sepulchral whisper to a crashing thunderclap." This "marvelous instrument" was "not of an organ or a trumpet, but rather of a trombone, the instrument possessing above all others the power to express the wide and varied range of emotions encompassed by the human voice — and with greater amplitude." During ecstatic moments, Johnson says, the preacher "strode the pulpit up and down in what was actually a very rhythmic dance." [2]

In the novel *Juneteenth*, Ellison's Rev. Hickman exploits, with a jazzy difference, the oratorical techniques of the old-time Negro preacher. The novelist Leon Forrest asked Ellison in 1972, "What is the process, the metamorphosis that goes into re-making a speech or sermon into art?" Ellison replied: "It is a blending of forms: church, congregation and drama. It is involved with rebirth and transcendence." [3] Ellison had been creating Hickman during the rise to prominence of Dr. Martin Luther King, Jr., and the height of popularity of the Reverend C. L. Franklin of Detroit, who traveled from city to city. Both Dr. King and Rev. Franklin drew upon the Negro preacher's relationship to the ritualized African American aesthetics of oration, as well as a specific tradition of Christian faith. "Christian" should not be read here in narrowly religious terms. Ellison himself continues this tradition. Rev. Hickman's sermon (first published in 1964) is inextricably linked to Dr. King's famous "I Have a Dream" speech of 1963 in Washington. Like the old-time Negro preacher who, Johnson says, "loved the sonorous, mouth-filling, ear-filling phrase," Rev. Hickman used words as elements of sound in their own right, notes on a scale beyond meaning and context.

In his book *The Preacher King: Martin Luther King and the Word That Moved America*, Richard Lischer focuses on King's "strategies of style," his use of such literary devices as alliteration, assonance, anaphora, and epistrophe, emphasizing how "King delighted in euphony." Lischer writes: "In a sermon on the Greeks who wished to see Jesus (in John 12), he [King] does not speak of Greek culture in the abstract but evokes the beauty of that culture by reciting the beautiful names of its greatest representatives: 'Aristophanes, Euripides, Thucydides, Demosthenes. . . .' And in the same sermon, King employs repetition for emphasis: 'Sir, we would see Jesus the light of the world. We know about Plato, but we want to see Jesus. We know about Aristotle, but we want to see Jesus. We know about Homer, but we want to see Jesus.'" [4] Ellison understood both the source and the nature of Dr. King's rhetorical virtuosity and the timeliness of his democratic vision. Dr. King, native son of Atlanta, brought the old-time Negro preacher's use of the performed word eloquently into play, thereby serving as public messenger, inspiring a nation, and urging it to allow, in the famous quote from his "I Have a Dream" oration, "justice to roll down like water and righteousness like a mighty stream."

Ellison was also well aware of the Reverend C. L. Franklin's singular oratorical gifts. He was the preacher-prince par excellence of the black Baptist circuit. Rev. Franklin was frequently broadcast live on black radio stations during the 1950s and 1960s, and his version of the "dry bones in the valley" was recorded for broadcast. In an interview Ellison commented on the "elegance" of Rev. Franklin's preaching.[5]

Jeff Todd Titon provides a source that may have had a direct impact on Ellison's creation of Hickman's preaching style. Titon says that Rev. Franklin "preached on several scripture passages repeatedly over the years; in so doing, he was like a poet or composer who continually revises his works,"[6] but Rev. Franklin's revisions are more immediately characteristic of the jazz musician's art of improvisation. The perpetual challenge for jazz musicians is to make an old song new. A "message" or vision is brought to the fore by making the familiar new — all the more effective because members of the audience can hear in the new rendition the essence of the old form.

Wynton Marsalis, a classical and jazz trumpeter, describes the inherent nature of the jazz musician's performance: "In jazz you [the performer] are the composer and the performer at the same time. So then you not only have the responsibility of virtuosity, you have the added responsibility of vision. And it is a lot easier to become a virtuoso than it is to have a vision. But you might have vision, and if you don't have the virtuosity, then you can't carry the vision forth."[7]

Rev. Hickman's sermon on "Juneteenth," an annual occasion in the South when blacks celebrate Lincoln's signing of the Emancipation Proclamation and the subsequent freedom of slaves, recalls a Sunday morning church service and its call-and-response ritual (with which the congregation is thoroughly familiar). He plays upon their willing indulgence of his rhetorical extravagance like a grand master playing a familiar anthem or hymn. His audience knows, for example, all about Ezekiel's vision of the wheel in the heavens; they know of the dry bones in the valley because they are dedicated students of the Bible. Yet they do not know *how* on this particular occasion he will perform, and that is why they have come out to hear him. Rev. Hickman, like any accomplished performer, is astutely attuned to his audience's expectations. He places his trombone on the piano as an early suggestion of things to come, a symbolic hint at poetic, even melodic, closure, a reminder of his improvisational relationship to his congregation. Like the jazz musicians who were always around him, Rev. Hickman knows that a genuine cathartic effect or transcendent meaning can only be achieved through virtuosity, imaginative flights of fancy, and inspired phrasing. In Rev. Hickman's Juneteenth sermon, virtuosity and vision are one.

Dry Bones in the Valley

Rev. Hickman, like Rev. Franklin, states the major themes or chords of his sermon at the outset, and then the members of his congregation are conveyed on solo flights of imagination, a journey made more wondrous by the sustained extemporaneous quality of the performance. Yet Rev. Hickman is not the only preacher in *Juneteenth*. Another is Bliss, the boy wonder who is to become the infamous Senator Sunraider. The Juneteenth sermon surfaces in the senator's consciousness as a repressed memory from his boyhood. Though his mode is retrospective ("Still I see it after all the roving years and flickering scenes"), his repressed and recovered memory comes back like a continuous dream. The senator was wounded during an assassination attempt. Hospitalized, he is in turn sharply conscious and then delirious. The Juneteenth episode, like others recalled during his delirium, has the vivid and alienated majesty of an old movie playing in the theatre of his own mind. We are taken back to a tent "beneath the pines," in a cleared open space "surrounded by trees," where he stands, merely six or seven years old, at one of "twin lecterns at opposite ends of the platform." Rev. Bliss is Rev. Hickman's Lilliputian sideman, playing vocal "piccolo" to Hickman's trombone voice. The delirious senator, seeing Daddy Hickman as a man "not so heavy then, but big with the quick energy of a fighting bull," sees as well "the battered silver trombone on top of the piano, where at the climax of the sermon he [Hickman] could reach for it and stand blowing tones that sounded like his own voice amplified; persuading, denouncing, rejoicing — moving beyond words back to the undifferentiated cry. In strange towns and cities the jazz musicians were always around him. Jazz. What was jazz and what religion back there?" [8]

Jazz, religion, and self-knowledge are inextricably linked in the wounded senator's mind. So is the question, despite his apparent resourcefulness, of self-delusion and charlatanism. Collective self-knowledge, the history of African Americans from slavery through Emancipation, is the primary purpose of the occasion, the congregation of five thousand Negroes gathered to celebrate Juneteenth. The "battered silver trombone" symbolizes Rev. Hickman's continued association with jazz musicians. It signals that jazz will be at the heart of the narrative and that Hickman's style of playing resembles that made famous by Joe "Tricky Sam" Nanton of Duke Ellington's orchestra, who perfected the "guttural" or "growl" style. In *Jazz Styles* Mark C. Gridley notes, "With his plunger and unorthodox blowing, Nanton came very close to pronouncing words with his trombone."[9] Daddy Hickman uses his trombone to bring poetic closure to his sermons. He creates "tones that sounded like his own voice amplified."[10]

At the outset, Rev. Hickman tells his congregation: "The Hebrew children have their Passover so that they can keep their history alive in their memories — so let us take one more page from their book and ... let us tell ourselves our story."[11] Throughout his sermon, Rev. Hickman is, at moments, professorial. He teaches his congregation their history. He sometimes makes learned allusions. Rev. Hickman's reference to the "Hebrew children" is a typical Ellisonian allusion to the unity in the diversity of American culture. African Americans, many of whom are avid students of the Bible, have seen their own slavery and freedom as a parallel to the plight of the Israelites who were trapped in bondage in Egypt, then lost in the wilderness, before they entered the Promised Land. Hickman's sermon, a history lesson of sorts, will also be "a happy occasion." Rev. Bliss agrees and acknowledges his assigned role: "They [the congregation] responded and I looked preacher-faced into their shining eyes, preparing my piccolo voice to support his [Rev. Hickman's] baritone sound."[12]

At this juncture, as in a live jazz performance, there is a sudden break — as though the musicians are heard playing an unexpected series of fleeting notes before returning to their major chords. The wounded and delirious senator, returning momentarily to consciousness, dreads his helpless plunge backwards into the black memory of things past: "*Not back to that me, not to that six-seven-year-old ventriloquist's dummy dressed in a white evening suit. Not to that charlatan born — must I have no charity for me?*"[13]

According to Rev. Hickman, "a true preacher is a kind of educator."[14] Rev. Hickman says to Rev. Bliss, almost tongue in cheek: "We come here out of Africa, son; out of Africa. Africa? Way over across the ocean? The black land? Where the elephants and monkeys and lions and tigers are? Yes, Rev. Bliss, the jungle land. Some of us have fair skins, like you, but out of Africa too." [15] Perhaps Ellison here recalls Countee Cullen's poem "Heritage," in which the speaker asks, "Africa? A book one thumbs / Listlessly, till slumber comes. / Unremembered are her bats / Circling through the night, her cats / Crouching in the river reeds, / . . . *One three centuries removed / From the scenes his fathers loved, / Spicy grove, cinnamon tree, / What is Africa to me?*" [16]

Rev. Hickman's statement about those Negroes with fair skins being out of Africa too, a characteristic Ellisonian use of wit and irony, alludes to intraracial hierarchy, and mockingly suggests that a caste system among Negroes based on "fair skin" is foolish. Hickman dispels the notion of Africa as the "the jungle land." Some Africans who arrived on American shores, he continues, "were the sons and daughters of heathen kings"; others were the sons and daughters of warriors, farmers, and "smelters of brass and iron." All came through the hell and torture of the transatlantic voyage, the Middle Passage. Hickman tells his congregation: "We went down into hell on those floating coffins and don't you youngsters forget it! Mothers and babies, men and women, the living and the dead and the dying all chained together." The sons and daughters of kings, warriors, farmers, musicians, and smelters of brass and iron were transformed into "nobody": "And they treated us like one great inhuman animal without any face. . . . Without personality, without names, Rev. Bliss, we were made into Nobody and not even Mister nobody either, just nobody. They left us without names. Without choice. Without the right to do or not to do, to be or not to be." Rev. Hickman alludes here to Hamlet's soliloquy about human resolution and resignation. [17] The sermon becomes "a parable," as the young Rev. Bliss calls it (begging for clarification in the process), and a dramatic recitation with the performed words taking on a poetic and musical life of their own.

Rev. Hickman tells Bliss: "They chopped us up into little bitty pieces like a farmer when he cuts up a potato. And they scattered us around the land. They scattered us around this land. . . . Like seed, Rev. Bliss; they scattered us like a dope-fiend farmer planting a field with dragon teeth!" [18] Here the planting of teeth alludes to Cadmus, of Greek mythology, who introduced writing to the Greeks and founded Thebes.

Daddy Hickman's sermon is a staged duet; his apprentice, the young Rev. Bliss, has been thoroughly tutored and responds like a true jazzman. He knows when to swing. He plays the role of Hickman's accompanist. He "comps" (as a pianist plays along while a soloist sings) by coming in and out as necessary, asking leading questions, repeating responses, and adding his own phrases here and there. He tells Daddy Hickman, the impassioned soloist, to speed up or slow down; using his piccolo repetitions and phrasings to answer Hickman's brassy call.

Rev. Hickman alludes to another devastating blow by the enslavers: "They scattered our tongues in this land like seed. . . . And left us without language. . . . They took away our talking drums." When Rev. Bliss responds in disbelief — "Drums that talked Daddy Hickman, tell us about talking drums" — Daddy Hickman answers with his own rhythmic exhortation: "Drums that talked like a telegraph. Drums that could reach across the country like a church bell sound. Drums that told the news almost before it happened! Drums that spoke with big voices like big men!"[19] He repeats the word "drums" at the beginning of each of eight sentences, and with the repetition achieves a percussive rhythm. It is characteristic of his virtuosity, but his vision also shines through. He spells out the many uses of the drums and the painful cultural loss when the drums were "burnt up," the silence of the talking drums symbolizing the destruction of collective languages and ritualistic ways of communicating and knowing. The drums "talked like a telegraph." They were vital instruments, necessary and ritualistic components of culture.

Daddy Hickman, with Rev. Bliss's assistance, begins "whooping" toward his climax. "Whooping" is a form of improvisational chanting, digression, repetition, and humming that moves considerably beyond a linear or coherent presentation of ideas, becoming an effortless transition to an expected and passionate rhetorical mode. Like Hickman, Rev. Franklin (according to Titon) "spoke during the first several minutes of a sermon in order to reach the hearers' intellect, then 'whooped' during the climax to reach their emotions."[20] Daddy Hickman's whooping, with Rev. Bliss comping in the background, uses a central theme, a rhythmic pattern of repetition, and a unique manner of phrasing to create exaggerated patterns of similarity, with added notes of difference: "I said, Rev. Bliss, brothers and sisters, that they snatched us out of the loins of Africa. I said they took us from our mammys and pappys and from our sisters and brothers. I said that they scattered us around this land. . . . And we were, let's count it again, brothers and sisters; let's add it up. Eyeless, tongueless, drumless, danceless, songless, hornless, soundless, sightless, dayless, nightless, wrongless, rightless, motherless, fatherless— scattered."[21]

Rev. Hickman's appeal to his congregation to "count it again, brothers and sisters," invokes the familiar call-and-response pattern that is as much a part of this ritual as his duet with Rev. Bliss. Having given his engaging call to his congregation, Rev. Hickman continues his counting, indeed his accounting, by calling upon Rev. Bliss's piccolo voice as a complement to his own trombone testimony: "Although we were ground down, smashed into little pieces; spat upon, stamped upon, cursed and buried, and our memory of Africa ground down into powder and blown on winds of foggy forgetfulness. . . . Amen! And God — Count it, Rev. Bliss." Bliss responds — counting the negatives and adding a few of his own. "Left eyeless, earless, noseless, throatless, teethless, tongueless, handless, feetless, armless, wrongless, rightless, harmless, drumless, danceless, songless, hornless, soundless, sightless, wrongless, rightless, motherless, fatherless, sisterless, brotherless, plowless, muleless, foodless, mindless, and Godless, Rev. Hickman, did you say Godless?"[22]

Hickman's virtuosity and staged arrangements (including the young Rev. Bliss's rehearsed repetitions) display his willingness to pull out all the stops. His calculated repetition of a varied series of negated nouns, emphasized over and over by the suffix "less," enhances the intensity of his whooping. His is a catalogue of negation — a swift and rhythmic accounting of losses endured by African Americans. Each catalogue — whether recited by Hickman or repeated by Bliss — begins with "eyeless," a suggestion of the bewildering complexity the new and "drumless" slaves faced in a strange land. "Eyeless" (I-less) has a double meaning also, suggesting a potential erasure of self-identity and cultural memory. And Daddy Hickman's repetitions also add mocking levity to the solemnity of his message. His repetition of negated nouns creates an ambience of tragicomic suspense, as the congregation is forced to wonder which negation, which "less," will surface next.

As Hickman speaks, mesmerizing his congregation with his account of losses, he musically dramatizes the physical and emotional death of many salves as well as the more general consequences of slavery. Yet the deaths of scattered and dismembered bodies ironically suggest reincarnation or reification of visionary possibility. That is, they suggest transcendence. The dead bodies will fertilize the American soil, which Rev. Hickman describes as "red and black like the earth of Africa," giving birth to new life.

Improvisation: Ellison Riffs on T. S. Eliot and Rev. C. L. Franklin

Rev. Hickman's whooping, like the jazz solos of Jimmy Rushing and Mahalia Jackson's gospel singing, evokes attitudes and values shared by the community. Like Jackson, who, Ellison says, "sings within the heart of the congregation as its own voice of faith," Daddy Hickman is at once playing upon and evoking a shared communal experience.[23] Therefore, when he talks of black bodies being "cut up" and "scattered like a dope-fiend farmer planting a field of dragon teeth," or "scattered around like seed," the preacher is leading his flock to his climax, to his transcendent metaphor of racial rebirth. The tale of rebirth and regrouping of Africans who become American Negroes is told with more emphasis and verve than the grim fable of enslavement and dismemberment. The catalogue of loss and negation, the missing body parts — "eyeless, earless, noseless, throatless, teethless, tongueless, handless, feetless, armless" — becomes a faint memory as skeletons are transfigured and reconnected, dry bone by dry bone. Rev. Bliss informs the congregation: "WE WERE LIKE THE VALLEY OF DRY BONES."

Ellison's sudden reference (via Hickman) to Ezekiel's dream, to the "valley of the dry bones," recalls T. S. Eliot's *The Waste Land* and reminds us, as Ellison did repeatedly, that Eliot's poem inspired him to begin a serious study of literature. Yet Ellison does not have a hierarchy of sources. The King James Bible, T. S. Eliot, and Rev. C. L. Franklin — high culture and the "elegance" of black Baptist fundamentalism — are all sources for his imaginative use and creative exploitation. In Ezekiel 37 the prophet tells of hearing God's voice: "And he said unto me, Son of man, can these bones live? . . . So I prophesied as I was commanded: and as I prophesied, there was a noise, and behold a shaking, and the bones came together, bone to bone." In *Juneteenth*, as Hickman's voice cries out to the dry Negro bones, Ellison deftly alludes to the "Burial of the Dead" section of

The Waste Land. Eliot's speaker says: "What are the roots that clutch, what branches grow/ out of this stony rubbish? Son of man, / you cannot say, or guess, for you know only / A heap of broken images, / where the sun beats, / And the dead tree gives no shelter, the cricket no relief, / And the dry stone no sound of water." [24] Rev. Hickman alludes to *The Waste Land* as the Negro bodies, symbolized by the "one nerve left," from "our ear . . . our feet . . . our heart," and so on (all pointed out dramatically by Rev. Bliss in a duet of racial affirmation and rebirth) begins "stirring . . . in the midst of all our death and buriedness": Hickman thunders out:

The voice of God spoke down the Word . . .

. . . Crying Do! I said, Do! Crying Doooo —

— these dry bones live?

He said: Son of Man . . . under the ground, ha! Heatless beneath the roots of plants and trees . . . Son of man, do . . .

I said, Do . . .

I said Do, Son of Man, Doooooo! —

— these dry bones live?

Amen! And we heard and rose up. . . . Ah, we sprang together and walked around. All clacking together and clicking into place. All moving in time! Do! I said, Dooooo — these dry bones live! [25]

Rev. C. L. Franklin also animates the bones in his version of "dry bones in the valley," giving dynamic contemporary levity to the eloquent solemnity of the King James rhetoric:

And then one morning
the valley begin to rumble . . .
Foot bone
was searching out an
ankle bone. . . .
And back bone
was joining to shoulder bone.
And shoulder bone
was tying in with neck bone.
And neck bone
was turning to head bone. [26]

As Hickman comes to the end of his sermon, he uses improvisation and variations on the biblical scripture and on other versions of

Ezekiel's vision of the valley of dry bones, including Rev. Franklin's. Ellison says Hickman "underwent an experience which turned him from his wild life as a musician into a serious minister, but one who also brought with him his experience as a showman. He isn't always sure when he's using religious methods, even though his motives are religious, or when he's allowing the devices of his old past to intrude."[27] Hickman goes a step or two beyond Rev. C. L. Franklin; since he knows all about the jazz musician's tricks of stage presence and presentation, his version of Ezekiel's vision involves Rev. Bliss acting out the dramatic scene of rebirth:

> And now strutting in my white tails, across the platform, filled with the power almost to dancing.
> Shouting, Amen, Daddy Hickman, is this the way we walked? . . .
> And him strutting me three times around the pulpit across the platform and back. Ah, yes! And then his voice deep and exultant: And if they ask you in the city why we praise the Lord with bass drums and brass trombones tell them we were rebirthed dancing, we were rebirthed crying affirmation of the Word, quickening our transcended flesh.[28]

Ellison's theme of transcendent rebirth is dramatically played out in terms that cannot be found in the King James Version of the Bible or in the animated anatomical spectacle of Rev. C. L. Franklin. Ellison's Negro race — via the "trombone" of Hickman's voice and Rev. Bliss's "strutting," his being "filled to the power almost to dancing" — is reborn in a jazzy scene stressing music and dance and ritualistic jubilation. Hickman brags about "bass drums and brass trombones." But Ellison rescues this scene from what appears to be a predictable aspect of religious charlatanism. The rebirth goes beyond the dancing and singing, the playing of bass drums, trombones. Daddy Hickman says: "We were rebirthed from the earth of this land and revivified by the Word. So now we had a new language and a brand-new song to put flesh on our bones. . . . New teeth, new tongue, new word, new song! We had a new name and a new blood, and we had a new task . . ."[29] The task probably refers to Henry James's famous lament that being an American was "an arduous task." Ellison connects the Negro's metaphorical and transcendent rebirth to the process of the United States' coming into its own as a nation. Daddy Hickman instructs his congregation: The new task is "to build up a whole new nation": "We had to use the Word as a rock to build up a whole new nation, cause to tell it true, we were born again in chains of steel. Yes, and chains of ignorance. And all we knew was the spirit of the Word. We had no schools. We owned no tools, no cabins, no churches, not even our own bodies." [30]

Ellison, Ellington, and Transcendence

Rev. Hickman sees the positive future of a "new nation" at the same time that he recalls and rephrases his catalogue of negation. Ellison maintains that "the marvelous and the terrible" are defining aspects of both African American history and the larger American experience. As Ellison says in "Blues People," "Any viable theory of Negro American culture obligates us to fashion a more adequate theory of American culture as a whole." Even in this context, Ellison alludes to the valley of the dry bones as he spells out his theory of the American cultural process: "The heel bone is, after all, connected, through its various linkages, to the head bone. Attempt a serious evaluation of our national morality and up jumps the so-called Negro problem. Attempt to discuss jazz as a hermetic expression of Negro sensibility and immediately we must consider what the 'mainstream' of American music really is." [31]

Daddy Hickman emphasizes the role the Word plays in the new nation; it is the new keynote. The Word is the embodiment of faith that inspires Hickman to instruct his congregation: "He [God] means for us to be a new kind of human." It is the Word found in Ezekiel's dreamy vision of the Hebrews rising to life from the dry bones in the valley, the Word of faith that made the dry bones live and breathe again. The Word in this context of building up a "whole new nation" suggests the treasured American documents to which Ellison often refers, the Declaration of Independence, the Bill of Rights, and the United States Constitution. (Ellison says in "Perspective of Literature": "I look upon the Constitution as the still vital covenant by which Americans of diverse backgrounds, religions, races, and interests are bound.") [32]

The climax of Rev. C. L. Franklin's sermon may have been Ellison's model. Rev. Franklin had invoked the Word as a compass against chaos:

Tell those bones,
"Hear my words."
And that's my solution tonight, . . .
Hear God's words. . . .
It's all right . . .
to call on scholars,
to call on businessmen. . . .
but I tell you what you had better do:
hear God's words,
hear God's words.
His words![33]

Rev. Franklin repeats in swift succession the phrases "God's word" or "His words" twenty-seven times, then sings several verses of a song: "I'm still counting on his word, I'm still leaning and leaning, and I'm still waiting and watching for his words."[34] Daddy Hickman ends on a different note. He reminds his congregation of the power of God's word: "We had to take the Word as food and shelter. We had to use the Word as a rock to build up a whole new nation," but at the climax of his sermon, the jazzman-turned-preacher blends in a secular note: "But we had the word, now, Rev. Bliss, along with the rhythm." He repeats "rhythm" nine times: "Keep to the rhythm and you'll keep to life. . . . Keep, keep, keep to the rhythm and you won't get weary. Keep to the rhythm and you won't get lost."[35] His words about rhythm are inspired by the words to one of Duke Ellington's famous songs, "It makes no difference if it's sweet or hot,/ Just keep that rhythm/ Give it everything you've got!/ It don't mean a thing/ If it ain't got that swing!"[36]

Hickman's final words to the congregation also involve rhythm and time: "There's been a heap of Juneteenths before this one and I tell you there'll be a heap more before we're truly free! Yes! But keep to the rhythm, just keep to the rhythm and keep to the way. . . . Time will come round when we'll have to be their eyes; time will swing and turn back around. I tell you, time shall swing and spiral back around."[37]

We spiral back to Senator Sunraider. The sermon is his repressed memory, returning in vivid cultural glory with all stops, inhibitions, and repression removed. His is a screen memory of sorts, a jazzy dream variation of the lost moments of his black and ambivalent childhood, including relics from his boyhood days — Hickman's battered silver trombone, his white tails, and, most significant of all, the trombone in Daddy Hickman's voice. He hears Daddy Hickman's words coming back with their original power and authority, blown back out of the "winds of foggy forgetfulness." [38]

Jazz Trumpet No End
Ellison's Riffs with Irving Howe and Other Critics

And his responsibility, which is also his joy and his strength and his life, is to defeat all labels and complicate all battles by insisting on the human riddle, to bear witness, as long as breath is in him, to that mighty, unnameable, transfiguring force which lives in the soul of man, and to aspire to do his work so well that when the breath has left him, the people — all people! — who search in the rubble for a sign or a witness will be able to find him there.
—James Baldwin, "Why I Stopped Hating Shakespeare"

Ralph Ellison: The *Yecke*

Ellison's critics, white and black, often call him arrogant and aristocratic. They point to his aloofness, reclusiveness — even his elegant suits and cigars have drawn negative attention. When Ellison is called an "elitist," his critics use his comments on the necessity of high artistic standards, of "stern discipline" and "excellence" in artistic execution, to validate their charge of aesthetic snobbery. When an interviewer asked him in 1965, "What do you consider the Negro writer's responsibility to American literature as a whole?" he responded: "The writer, any American writer, becomes basically responsible for the health of American literature the moment he starts writing seriously. . . . There is implicit in the act of writing a responsibility for the quality of the American language — its accuracy, its vividness, its simplicity, its expressiveness — and responsibility for preserving and extending the quality of the literature." [1] Ellison's critics hone in on comments of this sort.

In *Advertisements for Myself*, Norman Mailer says that Ellison's mind is "fine and icy" and concludes that "*Invisible Man* insists on a thesis which could not be more absurd, for the Negro is the least invisible of all people in America."[2] Norman Podhoretz, former editor of *Commentary* magazine, has criticized Ellison on several occasions. In "The Melting-Pot Blues," his review of Ellison's *Shadow and Act* for the *Washington Post*, Podhoretz calls Ellison's prose "knotted, graceless, pretentious," adding that most of the essays were "awkwardly composed, marred by pompous locutions, clumsy transitions and sometimes even bad syntax." He has a fundamental disagreement with Ellison over "pluralism." Ellison believes in the unity within the diversity of American culture. Podhoretz sees American culture in a different light: "The vision of a world in which many different groups live together on a footing of legal and social equality, each partaking of a broad general culture and yet maintaining its own distinctive identity: this is one of the noble dreams of the liberal tradition. Yet the hard truth is that very little evidence exists to suggest that such a pluralistic order is possible."[3]

Podhoretz likens the plight of American Negroes to that of American Jews and, unlike Ellison, believes that "the Negro subculture will disappear." He maintains that even the blues and jazz were "*produced by oppression.*" He comments on Ellison's stubborn refusal to agree: "Ellison is unwilling to believe — he is a stubborn man — that the things he values in the Negro subculture will disappear as Negroes win a greater and greater share of participation in the general society. . . . The price Jews have paid for acceptance in America . . . is the surrender of more than many Jews are by now even capable of realizing. I suspect that the Negroes will follow roughly the same pattern and be charged . . . roughly the same price."[4]

Furthermore, although in his memoir *Breaking Ranks* Podhoretz praises *Invisible Man* and sides with Ellison in his exchange with Irving Howe, he nevertheless found Ellison "pompous": "I found Ellison the man stuffy and pompous; he was in truth amazingly like one of the characters he himself satirized for those very qualities in *Invisible Man*. He also struck me as a Negro equivalent of certain prissy German Jews I knew (*yeckes*, in the derogatory Yiddish term for the type) who were forever preening themselves on their superior refinement, education, and culture."[5]

Ellison was also harshly criticized by various black writers for refusing to protest openly and to support the civil rights movement. When his name came up in 1965 at a conference on the black writer sponsored by the American Society of African Culture, the historian John Henrik Clarke summarily dismissed him. Ellison, he said, has spent "so much time in the last ten years in flight from his own people and has not even answered most mail addressed to him by his fellow black writers and has said positively that art and literature are not racial. He won't come into any Afro-American writer's conference."[6]

If Ellison often refused to attend conferences sponsored by African American writers, whether as a matter of aesthetic principle or personal taste, he also took public positions dissenting from certain white artists and writers. When in 1965 President Lyndon Johnson invited leading American writers, intellectuals, and artists to participate in a White House Arts Festival, many refused the invitation because of their opposition to the Vietnam War. Ellison attended. Afterward he criticized a letter (eventually published in various newspapers) that the poet Robert Lowell had written to President Johnson, objecting to the war. When Lowell's letter got to the press, Ellison called the circumstances and consequences "unfortunate." Lowell's refusal to attend, Ellison noted in "A Very Stern Discipline," amounted to "a political act, a political gesture." Ellison concluded: "The President wasn't telling Lowell how to write his poetry, and I don't think he's in any position to tell the President how to run the government."[7]

Some of Ellison's white colleagues accused him of having sold out to the establishment. He had reasons, however, for his attendance at the White House Arts Festival: "The incident forced me to realize once again that for all the values that I shared, and still share, with my fellow intellectuals . . . I had to accept the fact that if I tried to adapt to their point of view, I would not only be dishonest but would violate disastrously that sense of complexity, historical and cultural, political and personal, out of which it is my fate and privilege to write."[8]

Ralph Ellison and Irving Howe

Ellison expressed his perspective most forcefully in "The World and the Jug" and "Hidden Name and Complex Fate," his most notable essays of the 1960s. "The World and the Jug" has two parts, the first a sharp response to Irving Howe's essay "Black Boys and Native Sons" (*Dissent*, autumn 1963), published in the *New Leader* in December 1963; the second, a response to Howe's reply, appeared in the *New Leader*, on February 3, 1964. "Hidden Name and Complex Fate," a long and genial variation of "The World and the Jug," was an address sponsored by the Gertrude Clark Whittal Foundation at the Library of Congress on January 6, 1964. Considering the overlap between the publication dates of "The World and the Jug" and Ellison's delivery of "Hidden Name and Complex Fate," the Library of Congress address can be read as a long autobiographical footnote to his more polemical essay.

The epigrammatic titles of these essays are directly tied to Ellison's own life. "The World and the Jug" refers to a colorful saying out of the black pulpit. Whether used sincerely or mockingly, it suggests power and control. All women and men remain forever at the mercy of God's benevolent or vengeful hands, black preachers often say: God has "the world in a jug and the stopper in His hand!" Ellison's response to Howe adds rhetorical nuance: "Howe seems to see segregation as an opaque steel jug with the Negroes inside waiting for some black messiah to come along and blow the cork. . . . But if we are in a jug it is transparent, not opaque, and one is allowed not only to see outside but to read what is going on out there, and to make identifications as to values and human quality." [9]

When Ellison published "The World and the Jug," he was still the author of only one book, *Invisible Man*. (He had published many essays but *Shadow and Act*— 1964 — had not yet appeared.) Yet he was already a powerful figure in literary circles. *Invisible Man* had received both popular praise and critical acclaim. Howe had no apparent reason to criticize Ellison. In fact, Howe, Martha Foley, Howard Mumford Jones, and Alfred Kazin comprised the jury who chose *Invisible Man* for the National Book Award.[10] Ellison was really a secondary figure in Howe's essay. James Baldwin, whose controversial bestseller *Another Country* had been published the previous year, was Howe's primary subject. Wright and Ellison are brought in to round out the essay, the former as the courageous, if technically flawed, hero, the latter as the accomplished, though ideologically misguided, first novelist. By assessing the works of three major black writers of that period, Howe's essay was also intended to be, in part, a review of the state of black writing in the United States.

Perhaps Howe also felt that Baldwin's *The Fire Next Time* (1963) had received too much attention.[11] Baldwin's fiercely eloquent essay condemned much of American society and white racism, but, conciliatory in the end, it urged blacks and whites to come together "like lovers" and "achieve our country and change the history of the world."[12] Howe lumps Baldwin and Ellison together as talented but limited neophytes in the shadow of Richard Wright's militant naturalism. In "Black Boys and Native Sons," Howe claims: "The day *Native Son* appeared, American culture was changed forever. No matter how much qualifying the book might later need, it made impossible a repetition of the old lies. In all its crudeness, melodrama, and claustrophobia of vision, Richard Wright's novel brought out into the open, as no one ever had before, the hatred, the fear, and violence that have crippled and may yet destroy our culture."[13]

Howe concludes: "If such younger Negro novelists as Baldwin and Ralph Ellison were to move beyond Wright's harsh naturalism and toward more supple modes of fiction, that was possible only because Wright had been there first, courageous enough to release the full weight of his anger."[14] Howe is not prepared to understand the complex nature of Ellison's literary influences. Shortly after his arrival in New York, Ellison met Langston Hughes. Hughes lent Ellison his copy of André Malraux's *Man's Fate*. After reading the novel, Ellison quickly adopted Malraux as one of his literary "ancestors," whom, unlike a literary "relative" like Richard Wright, Ellison believes, "the artist is permitted to choose."[15]

Jerry Watts provides the most thorough and provocative discussion of the exchange that ensued between Howe and Ellison.[16] Watts, an African American critic, devotes almost half of his *Heroism and the Black Intellectual* to his analysis, explaining along the way the intellectual background and assumptions of Howe and Ellison while criticizing the general implications of the statements of both. Watts explains one source of Howe's critical passion: "While endorsing the victim status appeal for black writers, Howe was not acting hypocritically, for he essentially writes within a Jewish victim status syndrome," a fact "overlooked" in commentaries "intent on asserting that Howe advised black artists to act in ways different from white artists."[17]

Howe's fundamental error, as Ellison evidently viewed it, was his literary presumption. When Howe's essay appeared, Ellison was forty-nine, hard at work on his second novel. How could a critic of Howe's background presume to speak with such authority on all or (in Howe's words) "any Negro writer," or "the Negro world"? It did not matter to Ellison that some of Howe's comments about Baldwin and Wright are right on target. Howe also scores a subtle point about Ellison: "But even Ellison cannot help being caught up with the idea of the Negro. To write simply about 'Negro experience' with the esthetic distance urged by the critics of the fifties is a moral and psychological impossibility, for plight and protest are inseparable from that experience, and even if less political than Wright and less prophetic than Baldwin, Ellison knows this quite as well as they do." [18] Howe's comments actually echo some of Ellison's own words. In "The Art of Fiction," an interview conducted in 1955, Ellison was asked whether he considered his novel a purely literary work as opposed to one in the tradition of social protest. He responded: "I recognize no dichotomy between art and protest. Dostoevsky's *Notes from the Underground* is . . . a protest against the limitations of nineteenth-century rationalism; *Don Quixote, Man's Fate, Oedipus Rex, The Trial* — all these embody protest, even against the limitation of human life itself. . . . One hears a lot of complaints about the so-called 'protest novel,' especially when written by Negroes, but . . . the critics could more accurately complain about their lack of craftsmanship and their provincialism." [19]

Ellison found Howe's more sweeping assertions, his pronouncements about any and all Negro writers, let alone all black experience, wrong-headed. For instance, Howe had noted Wright's "searing experiences," viewing his hard life and the resulting prose as symbolic of all Negro writers and their writing: "For a novelist who has lived through the searing experiences that Wright has there cannot be much possibility of approaching his subject with the mature 'poise' recommended by high-minded critics. . . . Bigger Thomas may be enslaved to a hunger for violence, but anyone reading *Native Son* with mere courtesy must observe the way in which Wright, even while yielding emotionally to Bigger's deprivation, also struggles to transcend it. That he did not fully succeed seems obvious; one may doubt that any Negro writer can." [20]

Ellison considered Howe's comments outrageous. However harsh or genteel a writer's personal circumstances, he or she was still at the mercy of individual talent and vocational discipline. Ellison had praised the work of his friend the black artist Romare Bearden for his depiction of urban Negro life, the artist's ability to capture, in Ellison's phrase, the "mysterious complexity of those who dwell in our urban slums." [21] Ellison, while writing about the "searing experiences" of Negro life himself, had noted that often "the marvelous beckons from behind the same sordid reality that denies its existence." [22] Howe's view of black urban experience does not encompass

Ellison's and Bearden's sense of the paradoxes, let alone possibilities, present even in those unforgiving environments. When Howe refers to "the most degraded and inarticulate sector of the Negro world," he presumably has in mind the South Side of Chicago that Wright portrays, but he errs by robbing its inhabitants, not all of them "degraded" or "inarticulate," of their individuality. To Howe, Chicago's South Side and the nation's Harlems are apparently populated only by hapless, jobless, faceless people. He ignores the multifarious variety of human personalities. So, too, Howe's perspective cancels out the Ellisonian idea of transcendence personified, say, by Charlie Christian, the jazz guitarist who came from the segregated slums of Oklahoma City, and by another impoverished native son of Chicago, Benny Goodman.

In "The World and the Jug," Ellison responds to Howe's general pronouncements about "the Negro world": "One unfamiliar with what Howe stands for would get the impression that when he looks at a Negro he sees not a human being but an abstract embodiment of living hell. . . . He [the Negro] is a product of the interaction between his racial predicament, his individual will and the broader American cultural freedom in which he finds his ambiguous existence. Thus he too, in a limited way, is his own creation." Ellison informs Howe that Negro life has "its own insights into the human condition, its own strategies of survival"; and that the Negro has never been a "mere abstraction in someone's head." [23]

Ellison's comment that black Americans are more than their "racial predicament" is consistent with his own earlier and future statements. But Howe believes that Baldwin and Ellison soft-pedal the harshness of black life. Howe praises Ellison but also takes him to task: "Ellison writes with an ease and humor which are now and then simply miraculous. . . . He can accept his people as they are, in their blindness and hope — here, finally, the Negro world does exist, seemingly apart from plight or protest." But Howe finds *Invisible Man* nonetheless wanting, for its "implausible conclusion," a consequence, he concludes, of Ellison's "dependence on the post-war zeitgeist." It leads to "the sudden, unprepared and implausible assertion of unconditional freedom with which the novel ends." Howe refers here to Invisible Man's statement in the novel's epilogue that his world had become one of "infinite possibilities." Howe says that this statement "violates the reality of social life, the interplay between external conditions and personal will, quite as much as the determinism of the thirties. . . . Freedom can be fought for, but it cannot always be willed or asserted into existence. And it seems hardly an accident that even as Ellison's hero asserts the 'infinite possibilities' he makes no attempt to specify them." [24]

Despite Howe's comments about *Invisible Man*'s implausible conclusion, the novel as a whole, and especially its conclusion, remains more ambiguous and radical in its critique than Howe suggests. Indeed, few critics have recognized that *Invisible Man* is as violent and militant in its own way as *Native Son*. Bigger's two murders, gruesome and horrific as they are, are nevertheless the desperate acts of an isolated individual. There is more violence and blood in Ellison's novel. For instance, the prologue of *Invisible Man* opens with the protagonist butting "a tall blond man" who called him "an insulting name." He feels the man's "flesh tear and the blood gush out." The narrator butts and kicks him until he falls to his knees "profusely bleeding." The narrator then says: "Oh yes, I kicked him! And in my outrage I got out my knife and prepared to slit his throat, right there beneath the lamplight in the deserted street." [25] And in the final chapter, a race riot breaks out in Harlem. Unlike the black dwellers of Wright's South Side, who passively look on as the white police disrupt their lives and ransack their apartments in search of Bigger, the Harlemites loot, they burn, they steal, they shoot. Invisible Man participates, and he himself injures Ras the Exhorter, a flamboyant black nationalist community leader. There is blood running in the streets.

Howe actually says little about Ellison. He discusses what Negro writers may not be able to achieve; he criticizes what he considers to be *Invisible Man*'s overly optimistic conclusion; and he expresses his conviction that it was Richard Wright who had prepared the way for all Negro writers to come. Those three points serve as the launching pad for Ellison's fiery response. Ellison, it seems, was responding to Howe but speaking also to the literary elite of the nation, indeed the world— those intellectuals and writers who thought seriously about such matters. In that light, "The World and the Jug" is Ellison's assertion of his freedom of unique expression as an American writer, his freedom to use his imagination as an independent artist.

This was hardly the first time that an African American writer had taken such a stand. James Baldwin's essays — "Everybody's Protest Novel" (1948) and "Many Thousands Gone" (1949) — served as dramatic assertions of his literary intentions. Baldwin contradicted those who maintain that the Negro's "categorization alone . . . is real" and "cannot be transcended." [26] And long before Baldwin spoke out, Langston Hughes had made a similar pronouncement in his 1926 essay "The Negro Artist and the Racial Mountain": "We younger Negro artists who create now intend to express our individual dark-skin selves without fear or shame. If white people are pleased, we are glad. If they are not, it doesn't matter. We know we are beautiful. And ugly too. The tom-tom cries and the tom-tom laughs. If colored people are pleased we are glad. If they are not, their displeasure doesn't matter either. We build our temples for tomorrow, strong as we know how, and we stand on top of the mountain, free within ourselves." [27] Like Ellison, Hughes saw both the marvelous and the terrible in African American life.

Like Hughes standing "free" and defiant on the mountain top of his willful artistic ambition, Ellison insists on his individual artistic freedom despite the sociology of the black writer's existence. "The World and the Jug" is Ellison's considered response to a comprehensive set of critical assumptions and power for which Howe was an articulate representative. Ellison's essay can be appropriately read as an open letter of sorts, a public declaration of imaginative independence. African Americans — writers and others — could think for themselves. Howe serves as representative of a group of critics when, for instance, Ellison writes: "I could escape the reduction imposed by unjust laws and customs, but not that imposed by ideas which defined me as no more than the sum of those laws and customs. . . . I found some of the most treacherous assaults against me committed by those who regarded themselves as either neutrals, as sympathizers, or as disinterested military advisers." [28]

Howe had written that the black writer's existence "forms a constant pressure on his literary work, and not merely in the way that this may be true of any other writer, but with a pain and a ferocity that nothing could remove." [29] An African American writer presumably could never be free in the way a white writer could. Ellison, in reply, urges Howe to relinquish his "Northern white liberal version of the Southern myth of the absolute separation of the races": "No matter how strictly Negroes are segregated socially and politically, on the level of the imagination their ability to achieve freedom is limited only by their individual aspiration, insight, energy and will. Wright was able to free himself in Mississippi because he had the imagination and will to do so. He was as much a product of his reading as of his painful experiences, and made himself a writer by subjecting himself to the writer's discipline — as he understood it. The same is true of James Baldwin, who is not the product of a Negro store-front church but of the library, and the same is true of me." [30]

Ellison brings the library into what Howe considers the bleak landscape of segregated black life as a symbol of hope and inspiration. The library is an institution that transcended the limitations of particular cultures and individual circumstances. It is as well a special space symbolically linked to Wright's, Baldwin's, and Ellison's achievement of literary fame. Wright's *Black Boy* (1945), Baldwin's *Notes of a Native Son* (1955), and Ellison's *Shadow and Act* (1964) tell their respective stories as young bookworms. Ellison, writing about working at Tuskegee's library, makes his point: "So in Macon County, Alabama, I read Marx, Freud, T. S. Eliot, Pound, Gertrude Stein and Hemingway. Books which seldom, if ever, mentioned Negroes were to release me from whatever 'segregated' idea I might have had of my human possibilities. I was not freed by propagandists or by the example of Richard Wright. (I did not know him at the time and was earnestly trying to learn enough to write a symphony by the time I was twenty-six, because Wagner had done so and I admired his music), but by composers, novelists, and poets who spoke to me of more interesting and freer ways of life." [31] Similarly, Baldwin read all of the books in the Harlem branch of the New York Public Library and made his way down to the central Fifth Avenue library guarded, as he then viewed it, by two "majestic lions."

So too, in his autobiography, *Black Boy*, Wright tells how, with the assistance of a good white Catholic, he was able to check out (from a library reserved for whites only) H. L. Mencken's *Book of Prefaces* and *Prejudices*. Mencken's books gave Wright a veritable liberal-arts syllabus, a list of writers about whom he knew nothing: Conrad, Lewis, Anderson, Dostoevski, Flaubert, Maupassant, Tolstoy, Twain, Hardy, Crane, Zola, Norris, Gorky, Bergson, Ibsen, Shaw, Dumas, Poe, Mann, Dreiser, Eliot, Gide, Stendhal, among others. As Wright puts it, after "long years of semi-starvation," he "managed to keep humanly alive through transfusions from books." [32]

Ellison makes a similar point about Wright in "Richard Wright's Blues," (1945) his long review of *Black Boy* first published in the *Antioch Review*. He shows how themes found in Wright's autobiography echo and amplify similar matters found in a diverse range of other works: "As a non-white intellectual's statement of his relationship to Western culture, *Black Boy* recalls the conflicting pattern of identification and rejection found in Nehru's *Toward Freedom*. In its use of fictional techniques, its concern with criminality (sin) and the artistic sensibility, and in its author's judgment and rejection of the narrow world of his origin, it recalls Joyce's rejection of Dublin in *A Portrait of the Artist*. And as a psychological document of life under oppressive conditions, it recalls *The House of the Dead*, Dostoevsky's profound study of the humanity of Russian criminals." [33]

Ellison had, unlike Howe, a more immediate sense of Wright's literary ambition, the nature of his self-confidence, and the quality of his talent. He knew, for instance, of Wright's voracious reading of Joyce and Dostoevsky. When he was asked by interviewers whether he felt Wright "gauged his craft to the great writers of the world," Ellison replied: "He was constantly reading the great masters, just as he read the philosophers, the political theorists, the social and literary critics. He did not limit himself in the manner that many Negro writers currently limit themselves. And he encouraged other writers — who usually rebuffed him — to become conscious craftsmen, to plunge into the world of conscious literature and take their chances unafraid. He felt this to be one of the few areas in which Negroes could be as free and as equal as their minds and talents would allow." [34] Furthermore, in "Remembering Richard Wright," Ellison compared Wright's confidence (gained from Marxism) and his ambition to that of jazzmen: "He had the kind of confidence that jazzmen have, although I assure you that he knew very little about jazz and didn't even know how to dance. . . . Through his cultural and political activities in Chicago he made a dialectical leap into a sense of his broadest possibilities, as man and as artist. He was well aware of the forces ranked against him, but in his quiet way he was as arrogant in facing up to them as was Louis Armstrong in a fine blaring way." [35]

Yet even when Ellison understood and praised Wright as an artist and a man, he also saw his shortcomings, especially in light of Ellison's own literary aspirations. In "Remembering Richard Wright,"

Ellison defines a difference Howe was prepared neither to see nor to acknowledge. Ellison perceives in those same assumptions that Howe considers militant courage an aesthetic limitation: "For in my terms, Wright failed to grasp the function of artistically induced catharsis — which suggests that he failed also to understand the Afro-American custom of shouting in church. . . . Perhaps he failed to understand — or he rejected — those moments of exultation wherein man's vision is quickened by the eloquence of an orchestra, an actor or orator or dancer, . . . moments wherein we grasp, in the instant, a knowledge of how transcendent and how abysmal and yet affirmative it can be to be human beings. . . . The irony here is that Wright could evoke them, but felt, for ideological reasons, that tears were a betrayal of the struggle for freedom." [36]

These comments are characteristic of Ellison's overall artistic vision. He makes similar statements throughout his essays and interviews. In "The Art of Fiction," "A Very Stern Discipline," and "The Novel as a Function of Democracy," among other essays and interviews, he returns to the theme of the writer as communicator of the transcendent and affirmative. Furthermore, Ellison idealizes the jazz-like intensity of the moment when he refers to "the eloquence of an orchestra," and "moments of exultation" wherein the audience's "vision is quickened."

Ralph Ellison: The Grand Aesthetician

In "The Art of Fiction," Ellison provides a moving portrait of himself as a maturing artist, struggling to acquire vision and to master his craft: "At night I practiced writing and studied Joyce, Stein and Hemingway. Especially Hemingway; I read him to learn his sentence structure and how to organize a story. . . . I had been hunting since I was eleven, but no one had broken down the process of wing-shooting for me, and it was from reading Hemingway that I learned to lead a bird." [37]

In "Hidden Name and Complex Fate," Ellison moves beyond his portrait of the writer as a boy and a young man to consider his acquisition of technique. He says: "And when I say that the novelist is created by the novel, I mean to remind you that fictional techniques are not a mere set of objective tools, but something much more intimate: a way of feeling, of seeing and expressing one's sense of life. And the process of *acquiring* technique is a process of modifying one's responses, of learning to see and feel, to hear and observe, to evoke and evaluate the images of memory and of summoning up and directing the imagination." Ellison places the American novelist at the center of his discussion. He praises Melville, Twain, Hemingway, Fitzgerald, Faulkner, and Wright as exemplary writers "who lived close to moral and political problems." Such writers continue the most noble tradition of the American novel, which, Ellison says, "has borne, at its best, the full weight of the burden of conscience and consciousness which Americans inherit as one of the revolutionary circumstances of our national beginnings." [38]

From the start to the end of his literary career, Ellison articulated the responsibility of the American novelist. When in 1953 Ellison delivered "Brave Words for a Startling Occasion," his acceptance speech for being given the National Book Award, he spelled out what he himself tried to accomplish while writing *Invisible Man*. He writes partly to correct what he calls the "unrelieved despair" ("except for the work of William Faulkner") of American fiction of the late 1940s and early 1950s: "I was to dream of a prose which was flexible, and swift . . . , confronting the inequalities and brutalities of our society forthrightly, yet thrusting forth its images of hope, human fraternity and individual self-realization." Ellison would "use the richness of our speech, the idiomatic expression and the rhetorical flashes from past periods" to "arrive at the truth about the human condition . . . with all the bright magic of a fairy tale." [39]

Thirty years after the National Book Award and twenty years after "Hidden Name and Complex Fate," Ellison elaborates upon the "interests of art and democracy" in the introduction he wrote for the thirtieth anniversary edition of *Invisible Man* (1982): "Here it would seem that the interests of art and democracy converge, the development of conscious articulate citizens being an established goal of this democratic society." "The novelist," Ellison explains, "seeks to create forms in which acts, scenes and characters speak for more than their immediate selves." He notes that despite the nation's racial problem "human imagination is integrative," and "the same is true of the centrifugal force that inspirits the democratic process." [40] Clearly, some of the same issues that he discussed in "Hidden Name and Complex Fate" and in "The World and the Jug," his exchange with Irving Howe, are still on his mind two decades later.

Ralph Ellison: The Elitist?

In *Heroism and the Black Intellectual: Ralph Ellison, Politics, and Afro-American Intellectual Life*, Jerry Watts isolates what he considers a central weakness in Ellison's response to Howe. Ellison inappropriately disregards "the material world" as a crucial factor in African American life: "To Ellison, any theory or argument that purports to have discovered unique boundaries and finite consistencies to the ways that blacks think, feel, or act is too restrictive to capture Negro humanity. The material world, according to Ellison, has a drastically limited impact on the lives of people. It is merely the setting upon which people act. Howe's social determinism, as well as his views concerning the suffering and anger of the Negro that led him to advocate a quasi-straitjacket of protest for the Negro writer, were Marxian influenced. Ellison, in challenging Howe on this point, wanted to challenge all social deterministic theories, not simply Marxian."[41]

Although Watts concedes that Ellison makes a valid point in maintaining that blacks are "more than victims," he says Ellison is given to "romanticizing a bleak situation." Watts refers to Ellison's comments about Wright's most famous character, Bigger Thomas: "Hidden behind Ellison's desire to proclaim potential human mastery over any social situation is also the claim that social situations are seldom as desperate as social scientists depict them. In hopes of portraying the richness, depth, and diversity of black life, Ellison tinkers with rendering epiphenomenal much of the oppression of blacks. . . . Ellison has argued that Wright could imagine a Bigger Thomas but Bigger could not have imagined Richard Wright. . . . Ellison could not admit . . . that there are thousands if not tens of thousands of blacks like Bigger Thomas who could not and cannot imagine a Richard Wright."[42]

What does Watts mean when he speaks of Ellison's "romanticizing a bleak situation"? "Ellison's folk pastoralism," Watts writes, "celebrates blacks for singing the blues and creating jazz, but he concertedly overlooks those aspects of the black folk culture that view it as a source of pride to pistol-whip women, to kill someone in a cold-blooded manner, to father numerous children without concern for their upbringing, or to pimp women."[43] As Watts sees it, Ellison ignores the Bigger Thomases — the outlaws and thugs — of black life. As we already have seen in "Harlem Is Nowhere," among other essays, Ellison focuses on "the marvelous" *and* "the terrible" in African

American life — one of his central themes. Indeed he stresses the marvelous as a corrective to the overwhelming emphasis by journalists, statisticians, politicians, and certain intellectuals on blacks as criminals or victims — "an abstract embodiment of living hell," in the phrase that Ellison used when responding to Irving Howe.

Watts argues that Ellison — the "elitist" — is "out of touch" with the black masses. Ellison "writes/speaks as if Harlem is alive with blacks who sing the blues or dance to jazz bands. Today most blacks are subjected to popular culture. Mass-marketed artifacts such as Janet Jackson, Grover Washington, Michael Jackson, Bill Cosby, and Mr. T. have very little to do with a distinct, organic ethnic folk culture, theirs or anyone's. Not only does Ellison romanticize Afro-American folk culture, weeding out arbitrarily that which he does not like, but his notion of folk culture also stands outside time and social influences." [44] Watts makes an excellent point about the atemporal quality of some of Ellison's statements on African American culture. But Ellison was hardly out of touch since, unlike Baldwin or Wright, he lived near Harlem until his death. And since he was one on whom nothing was lost, he clearly recognized that jazz was no longer the institution it once was, when Harlemites were swinging at Minton's Playhouse or stomping at the Savoy.

Ellison might respond to Watts's fine point about the mass-marketing of Michael Jackson and Bill Cosby by pointing out that each may have affected Madison Avenue at least as much as it transformed and packaged them. Put another way, Ellison would remind Watts of what he calls the "deceptive metamorphoses" in American culture, the ongoing "blending of identities, values and life styles" that define and shape the country as we know it. And the novelist might ask Watts which came first, the entrepreneurial chicken or the definitive egg? Did the mass-marketers teach Michael Jackson how to sing and dance, or did that come from his native Gary, Indiana, or his studious observation, as he and his four brothers waited in the wings, of James Brown's spinning, sliding, and camel-walking on stage? And might not Bill Cosby have learned something about the timing and delivery of his jokes from earlier black comedians such as Redd Fox and Pigmeat Markham? And it goes without saying that, despite Madison Avenue and because of it, Harlem still has some of what it had during the 1920s — rhythm, style, bold colors, and a sense of life as urban drama. Recall Invisible Man's assertion that Harlemites still speak "a jived-up transitional language full of country glamour, think transitional thoughts though they dream the same old ancient dreams."

Watts's study of Ellison has an inherent conceptual limitation. His characterization of Ellison as *merely* an intellectual is flawed. Ellison is not only an intellectual in the classic sense, one who possesses a dispassionate interest in ideas for their own sake, but he is also an artist who believes in the imagination's freewheeling creativity and extravagance. One must take into account his formidable intellect as well as his playful imagination — the former leading in "The World and the Jug" to his captious exchange with Howe, the latter to *Juneteenth* and Rev. Hickman's sonorous evocation of "the dry bones in the valley."

Howe behaves in a similar critical manner in reducing *Invisible Man* to manageable ideological proportions. The novel, he feels, lacks "the clenched militancy" of Wright's *Native Son*. He takes the narrator's statement in the epilogue — "My world has become one of infinite possibilities" — as the novel's and Ellison's bottom line. Howe gets it half right. This confidence and infinite hope is Ellison's. But his final position, despite Invisible Man's optimistic assertions, is ambiguous. Ellison leaves us with his dramatization of invisibility, in which one is seen but not seen, as a curse and a blessing. In the end, we are left to ponder the tragicomic nature of American life, the ironies, contradictions, the social absurdities of racial arrangements, the ambiguities of the racial situation in the United States.

Watts also criticizes Ellison for "heroic individualism" and even reads "The Charlie Christian Story" as Ellison's studied attempt to celebrate the genius while forgetting the genius's "poor neighbors": "Ellison is rhetorically willing to silence the pain and desperateness of Charlie Christian and his poor neighbors simply because of Christian's musical genius that evidently gave these people their voice. His concern is less with the folk but with the heroic individual who comes out of the folk and renders their suffering meaningful." [45] To the contrary, Ellison's essays, including "The Charlie Christian Story," relentlessly attempt to rescue and restore the complexity of the image of African Americans from those determined to see only walking personifications of crime and pathology, or victims of the unforgiving "material world." Ellison always recognizes "the marvelous" and "the terrible." In "The Charlie Christian Story," he writes of the slum —

full of "poverty, crime and sickness" but also "alive and exciting" — in which Christian flourished.[46]

Watts continues his critique of Ellison as an elitist, focusing on his supposed unwillingness to defend or to help improve the plight of poor and suffering African Americans; he ponders too whether the achievement of Duke Ellington and Louis Armstrong would have been diminished or enhanced by lives of active social protest. What if, Watts wonders, they had spent "enormous amounts of time and energy on picket lines protesting the racism they had to confront as American jazz musicians? Might their music have suffered? Might their music have benefited from the better treatment they may have received as a result of walking picket lines?" Watts concedes that as Ellison views it, Armstrong, Ellington, and others did protest injustice "through their art." Yet, Watts asserts, "someone had to engage in the concerted struggle to improve the status of jazz musicians in the United States. . . . Who were these people?" Watts gives some weight to both sides of the question, but nonetheless concludes that neither Armstrong nor Ellington "received better treatment because of their music skills."[47]

Ralph Ellison, through his role as a custodian of culture, wrote seminal essays on jazz — on Charlie Christian, Louis Armstrong, Duke Ellington, Charlie Parker, Jimmy Rushing, and others for popular magazines like Saturday Review, Esquire, and High Fidelity. Ellison, in effect, created his own picket line of the mind, one that raised the public's awareness about the lives and music of jazz musicians. So, too, through their music, Ellington and Armstrong influenced the nation's slow progress toward social equality. Armstrong's visit to Oklahoma City brought out young white women to the segregated black section and Ellington's tour of the South had a similar impact. Their music inspired some whites to move beyond southern expectations of law and custom.

Whatever one ultimately makes of Ellison's "heroic individualism," his view of the melting pot, of "deceptive metamorphoses," of whites being "part Negro without even knowing it," he made those statements at a most unlikely historical moment. He was willing to express strong dissent in the interest of cultural and historical accuracy. During the 1960s, he could have readily accepted the fashionable view of racial pride. Many black Americans were emphasizing, even exaggerating, all that was culturally distinct. It was the heyday of the Afro or the "natural" hairstyles worn by black students, celebrities, and politicians. The word "Negro" became overnight a nominal badge of oppression and subservience. It was abruptly jettisoned and "black" became the preferred adjective and noun. Blacks or black Americans believed in "black pride," "black power," and "black self-determination." "Black is beautiful" became a mantra. And "Blackness is a state of mind" became a militant slogan. Departments and programs dedicated to black studies were organized at colleges and universities. Ellison stuck to his guns, continuing to use "Negro" for a long time after such usage was considered passé.

Ralph Waldo Ellison:
Jazz Artist and Metaphysical Rebel

Ellison was "politically incorrect" before the phrase was coined. Considering the temper of the times, his was not an easy position for him to take or for others to endorse. In a superficial way, his vision appears conservative because he emphasizes democratic unity and harmony. Yet he readily points out that whatever unity is achieved is problematic. He eschews nonetheless the rhetoric of racial separation, even when victims of racism champion it. He argues that on the deepest level, where culture is really made — the way specific groups of people make moral choices, think, talk, and play — the integrative nature of democratic culture asserts itself most forcefully. His view transcends the definition of acculturation in which culture is seen to pass in a neat hierarchical manner from a supposedly civilized white population to relatively untutored African Americans. For instance, he believes that black slaves taught, influenced, and transformed their white masters at least as much as their masters taught and changed them.

For liberals, white and black alike, the Ellisonian perspective complicates the notion of blacks as perpetual victims of racial discrimination. The notion of the melting pot's refusing to melt validates the superficial notion that skin color and the social "integration" of African Americans — their admission to predominantly white colleges and universities, their residence in white neighborhoods, their attendance at white or integrated churches — was all that the melting pot was really about. The liberal confusion of social integration with profound and fundamental cultural exchange ruled out Ellison as a persuasive representative in the militant and racialized climate of the 1960s.

Black nationalists, let alone separatists, saw Ellison at worst as a traitor and at best as a misguided conciliatory "Negro" advocate of the status quo. Ellison's ongoing insistence on taking into account the complexity and ambiguity of America's democratic milieu and his emphasis on the resilience and monumental resources of the human will — its inherent yearning for freedom and expression — were anathema to black nationalists. Ellison's response, for instance, to the assertion of then Leroi Jones, later self-named Amiri Baraka, that "a slave cannot be a man" is characteristic of his stance. In his review of Jones's *Blues People* in the *New York Review of Books* (1964), Ellison asks Jones a series of questions:

> But what, one might ask, of those moments when he feels his metabolism aroused by the rising of the sap in spring? What of his identity among other slaves? With his wife? And isn't it closer to the truth that far from considering themselves only in terms of that abstraction, 'a slave,' the enslaved really thought of themselves as *men* [and women] who had been unjustly enslaved? And isn't the true answer to Mr. Jones' question, 'What are you going to be when you grow up?' not, as he gives it, 'a slave' but most probably a coachman, a teamster, a cook, the best damned steward on the Mississippi, the best jockey in Kentucky, a butler, a farmer, a stud, or, hopefully, a free man! Slavery was a most vicious system and those who endured and survived it a tough people, but it was *not* and this is important for Negroes to remember for the sake of their own sense of who and what their grandparents were, a state of absolute repression.[48]

It is unlikely that any other American writer of Ellison's generation would have, in 1964, been writing anything like Ellison's review for the pages of the *New York Review of Books*. His view is not "politically correct," in the sense of loyalty to any set of prescribed or understood assumptions. By removing the slave beyond a definition of utter victimization to a complex sense of transcendent human experience and possibility, he sees slavery as an ambiguous human situation, a "peculiar institution" indeed. The slave system cannot be completely understood by morally condemning the oppressive white masters and pointing out the moral superiority of the victimized slave. Slaves, men and women, were more than the sum of their brutalization. The comprehensiveness, indeed the theoretical perspective implicit in Ellison's critique, is unique in its lack of compromise, its unwillingness to accept fashionable militant or liberal rhetoric as a substitute for awkward and difficult human truths. Ellison, unlike Jones, views the male slave as fully in possession of his manhood, though a slave, and therefore privy to and inescapably a part of the glory and the effects of spring. Slaves, like all other humans, are partly defined by their interactions with others — other slaves, masters, relatives and friends — no less than by their personal talents and desires, by public demands and private dreams. Slaves, to use Ellison's own words, are "*below* the threshold of social hierarchy," but remain principal American players "existentially right in the middle of the social drama."[49]

What Ellison's critics, white and African American, have failed to either acknowledge or understand is how relentlessly dedicated he was to clarifying the profound influence of black life in America. He consistently views his role as a black artist to capture "the terrible" — the pain and oppression — but also the "marvelous" — the joy and laughter. In "A Very Stern Discipline," he says: "Yes, and I *must* affirm those unknown people who sacrificed for me. I'm speaking of those Negro Americans who never knew that a Ralph Ellison might exist. . . . I am forced to look at these people and upon the history of life in the United States and conclude that there is another reality behind the appearance of reality which they would force upon us as truth."[50]

To Ellison, other African American artists also have a responsibility to dedicate themselves to discover, portray, and indeed proclaim the accurate, though ambiguous, African American "reality behind the appearance of reality." "What is missing today," Ellison asserts, "is a corps of artists and intellectuals who would evaluate Negro American experience from the inside. . . . Rather, we depend upon outsiders — mainly sociologists — to interpret our lives for us. It doesn't seem to occur to us that our interpreters might well be not so much prejudiced as ignorant, insensitive, and arrogant."[51]

To critics like Howe and Watts, Ellison remains an elitist. And what Watts identifies as a partial source of Ellison's elitism is troubling. Watts raises his most challenging questions in the context of what

Ellison calls his "notorious" second novel: "As heroic individualist, Ellison appears to be tormented by his ambitions. The Achilles' heel of heroic individualism is unrealistic, almost obsessive-compulsive, artistic ambition. Certainly, there is something obsessive-compulsive about Ellison spending forty years writing a second novel." Watts speculates, regarding such a prolonged gestation period, that "a metaphorical, unsatisfiable 'great white master' may have taken up residence in Ellison's black superego. If this is the case, Ellison's unique bid to escape the parochialism of racist America may have led him into one of racism's most pernicious traps, an overbearing self-doubt." [52]

It remains difficult in the end to respond fully to Watts's criticism. Even before the fire in 1967 that destroyed a substantial portion of the manuscript, Ellison had trouble bringing *Juneteenth* to poetic closure. Why? Perhaps the stunning success and power of *Invisible Man* led to the eventual posthumous publication of *Juneteenth*. Seldom if ever discussed is the widespread sense of Ellison as a one-book wonder. This view ignores Ellison's full talent, and, indeed, his production. He wrote and published consistently for almost fifty years. The volume of his collected essays runs to more than 850 pages with over 60 essays. *Flying Home*, a volume of his posthumously published early stories, has become a part of his legacy. And *Juneteenth* will haunt the literary world well into the future. Nonetheless, the question remains: why couldn't Ellison achieve the grand finale he clearly yearned for by bringing his "notorious" second novel to the light of day during his lifetime? Was he thwarted, as Watts suggests, by a "great white master" inside his head?

Norman Podhoretz seems to have read Watts. After the publication of *Juneteenth*, Podhoretz's essay "What Happened to Ralph Ellison" appeared in *Commentary* in 1999. Among other salient comments, Podhoretz rehearses the reasons for his personal dislike of Ellison; he speculates on Ellison's possible envy of James Baldwin (though he provides no credible evidence); he explains why he no longer considers *Invisible Man* a great novel; and he says that Ellison suffered from a peculiar strain of writer's block. He also refers to what, by his own admission, was his "wrong-headed negative review" of Ellison's essay collection *Shadow and Act*, saying that despite the "stilted and awkward and pretentious" prose of Ellison's essays, they have "acquired a luminosity and nobility." He concludes by hailing Ellison, not as a great novelist (given that *Invisible Man* is "overrated" and *Juneteenth* is "half-baked"), but as "a magnificent intellectual and moral and political exemplar."[53]

Podhoretz also names the "great white master" that Watts believes was inside Ellison's psyche:

> Other parts of the 2,000-page manuscript he left behind may prove me wrong, but for now my speculation is that Ellison — a man of great intelligence and literary erudition who had an ear second to none — knew that Faulkner had invaded and taken him over and that this was why he could never finish the book. I can imagine him struggling for 40 years to get Faulkner's sound out of his head; I can imagine him searching desperately for the lost voice he had created in *Invisible Man*; I can imagine him trying to fool himself into thinking that he had finally found it again, and then realizing that he had not; and I can imagine him being reduced to despair at this literary enslavement into which some incorrigible defect in his nature had sold him — and to a Southern master, at that![54]

Podhoretz identifies Watts's so-called "great white master" and views Faulkner as "the ghost haunting the prose" in *Juneteenth* — thereby reducing Ellison to "literary enslavement."

However seductive Podhoretz's notion may be, it is essentially an academic fantasy. It echoes Harold Bloom's famous theory of the seventies — "the anxiety of influence." But it is hardly grounded in reality. To be sure, Ellison's respect for and indeed admiration of Faulkner as a novelist, as Podhoretz notes, is hardly a secret. But Ellison quickly sized up Faulkner as a novelist and a man. After Faulkner wrote his famous letter to *Life* magazine advocating that northern liberals slow down their desegregation activities, Ellison wrote to his friend Albert Murray from Rome on March 16, 1956:

> Faulkner has delusions of grandeur because he really believes that he invented these characteristics which he ascribes to Negroes in his fiction and now he thinks he can end this great historical action [desegregation] just as he ends dramatic action in one of his novels with Joe Christmas dead and his balls cut off by a man not nearly as worthy as himself; Hightower musing, the Negroes scared, and everything just as it was except for the brooding, slightly overblown rhetoric of Faulkner's irony. Nuts! He thinks

that Negroes exist simply to give ironic overtone to the viciousness of white folks, when he should know very well that we're trying hard as hell to free ourselves; thoroughly and completely, so that when we got the crackers off our back we can discover what we [Negroes] really are and what we really wish to preserve out of the experience that made us.[55]

In fairness to Watts, it must be noted that his book was published years before the appearance of *Juneteenth*. Furthermore, Watts took the matter beyond the immediate "literary enslavement" theory in the sense of a single "great white master." Watts connects Ellison's "obsessive-compulsive" relationship to the art of his fiction to the writer's supposed elitism. While Ellison may have been difficult to get to know, he was by no means elitist in the usual sense of the word. Unlike Henry James, Richard Wright, and James Baldwin, who became expatriates, he spent his whole life in New York City's Washington Heights, a few blocks from Harlem. He celebrates the achievement of black folklore in the same respectful tone he uses for the work of the more usual great masters of literature: "But what we've achieved in folklore has seldom been achieved in the novel, the short story, or poetry. In the folklore we tell what Negro experience really is. We back away from the chaos of experience and from ourselves, and we depict the humor as well as the horror of our living. We project Negro life in a metaphysical perspective and we have seen it with a complexity of vision that seldom gets into our writing."[56] Ellison also sees in American popular culture, including sports, something about "the nature of possibility" and a certain revelatory and transformative power: "Literary people should always keep a sharp eye on what's happening in the unintellectualized areas of our experience. . . . Because while baseball, basketball, and football players cannot really tell us how to write our books, they *do* demonstrate where much of the significant action is taking place. Often they are themselves cultural heroes who work powerful modification in American social attitudes." Ellison also speaks of the "Picasso-like experimentation" and "sense of creative power" found among many "Negro athletes."[57]

In his article "Ellison's Zoot Suit," first published in *Black World*, the critic Larry Neale succinctly captures the form and quality of Ellison's "radical" achievement when he concludes that Ellison's writing represent a true "black aesthetic": "Ellison . . . finds the aesthetic all around him. . . . He finds it in preachers, blues singers, hustlers, gamblers, jazzmen, boxers, dancers, and itinerant storytellers. He notes carefully the subtleties of American speech patterns. He pulls the covers off the stereotypes in order to probe beneath the surface where the hard-core mythic truth lies. He keeps checking out style. The way people walk, what they say and what they leave unsaid. If anyone has been concerned with a 'black aesthetic' it has certainly got to be Ralph Ellison." [58]

Ellison, like an accomplished jazz virtuoso, would take from the great masters — black or white — and improvise, extending their art as he creates his own. He says in "A Completion of Personality" that Joyce and Eliot "made me aware of the playful possibilities of language. You look at a page of *Finnegans Wake* and see references to all sorts of American popular music; yet the context gives it an extension from the popular back to the classical and beyond." [59] Ellison's allusion to American popular music suggests a possibility (related to his writer's block) at least as plausible as Watts's great-white-master speculation or Podhoretz's literary-enslavement conclusion. What if Ellison worried more about black artistic masters instead of white ones? What if he dreamed of achieving (not once as in the case of *Invisible Man* but again and again) what Bearden had been able to paint and capture in his collages and what Ellington had been able to play in his music? The theory that black artists, especially jazz masters, were looking over Ellison's shoulder is as compelling as any regarding a white master. And perhaps there is another reason he failed to arrive at poetic closure. What if that black jazz master was Ellison himself? What if he was his own worst enemy, like a mentor demanding — beyond boundaries of race, class, and nation — such exalted and bewildering standards of artistic originality that fulfillment was impossible?

Around the time that he sent *Invisible Man* to the printer, in June of 1951, Ellison wrote Albert Murray a letter that is germane to our present discussion. Ellison tells Murray that he had been having trouble with his transitions until he saw in page proofs the straightforward transitions of a friend's novel: "What I needed to realize was that my uncertainty came from trying to give pattern to a more or less raw experience through the manipulations of imagination, and that same imagination which was giving the experience new form, was also (and in the same motion) throwing it into chaos in my own mind. I had chosen to recreate the world, but like a self-doubting god, was uncertain that I could make the pieces fit smoothly together. Well, it's done now and I want to get on to the next."[60] Perhaps we should label Ellison's writer's block the "self-doubting god" syndrome.

Furthermore, in a little-known essay called "Why I Stopped Hating Shakespeare," James Baldwin grappled with a similar dilemma: "My quarrel with the English language has been that the language reflected none of my experience. . . . If the language was not my own, it might be the fault of the language; but it might also be my fault. . . . If this were so, then it might be made to bear the burden of my experience if I could find the stamina to challenge it, and me, to the test." Baldwin then names his sources of support and inspiration: "I had two mighty witnesses: my black ancestors, who evolved the sorrow songs, the blues and jazz, and created an entirely new idiom in an overwhelmingly hostile place; and Shakespeare, who was the last bawdy writer in the English language."[61]

Whether Ellison's supposed anxiety was fueled by white masters, black masters, jazz masters, or his own idiosyncratic self-doubt does not really matter in the end. An impenetrable mystique surrounds great artists, as *artists*, during their lives and long after their deaths. Critics, like detectives, are driven to discover the identity of their creative muses and demons. Yet tracking down the myriad demons that thwart the creativity of individual writers, let alone artists in general, remains a risky exercise.

The usual labels — elitist, conservative, aristocratic — used to describe Ellison do not help us unravel the mystery of what he once referred to as "his slow tempo of creation." In preceding chapters, we referred to him as a "metaphysical rebel." This phrase surfaces in *Invisible Man*. When one looks closely at his essays, interviews, *Invisible Man*, and *Juneteenth*, Ellison is, in crucial ways, unsparing in his critique of American life. When, for instance, he reflects upon the actions and motives of the Founding Fathers at Philadelphia and the negative consequences of what he refers to as their "failure of nerve," he concludes: "The Founding Fathers committed the sin of American racial pride. They designated one section of the American people to be the sacrificial victims for the benefit of the rest. . . . Indeed, they

[African Americans] were thrust beneath the threshold of social hierarchy and expected to stay there." [62]

We have also noted how the Harlem riot and Invisible Man's response to it reveal a side of Ralph Ellison that is rarely discussed —
the subversive within the artist. When Invisible Man confronts Ras,
the black nationalist community leader, during the Harlem riot, one
hears in the protagonist's words a reflection of Ellison's general artistic stance pushed through to a laserlike, militant logic: "I faced them
knowing that the mad man in a foreign costume was real and yet unreal, knowing that he wanted my life, that he held me responsible for
all the nights and days and all the suffering and for all that which I
was incapable of controlling. . . . And that I, a little black man with an
assumed name, should die because a big black man in his hatred and
confusion over the nature of a reality that seemed controlled solely by
white men whom I knew to be as blind as he was just too much, too
outrageously absurd. And I knew that it was better to live out one's
own absurdity than die for that of others, whether Ras's or Jack's." [63]

Ellison chose to live out his own absurdity, as some of his critics
and detractors may see it. In "Cadillac Flambé" he creates Lee Willie
Minifees, who maintains his own high standards as a musician and a
citizen. He listens to various jazz masters — Duke Ellington, Dinah
Washington, and Coleman Hawkins — and studies their phrasing,
and he wants to drive the best car Americans produce. As his Cadillac
burns on Senator Sunraider's lawn, he tells the stunned onlookers
that he purchased a Cadillac because "all he wanted was the best."
Minifees's sacrifice of his automobile was a radical gesture, one that
even McIntyre, the white reporter-narrator, observes was "so extreme
a reply as to be almost metaphysical." [64]

In *Juneteenth*, Rev. Hickman's closing words about discipline and
his philosophical answer to Bliss's question about identity — "who
we are" — represent the final striking of familiar Ellisonian chords.
When Hickman says to Bliss and the congregation, "We know where
we are by the way we walk," he implicitly connects identity to geogra-
phy or place. He initially rephrases "who" as "where" and thereby sees
inscribed in the African American's collective habits of being—walking, talking, singing, praying — the complex fate of African Americans as well as that of the United States, which Rev. Hickman calls
"a whole new nation." This connection brings to the fore another

familiar Ellison theme, the impossibility of imagining the United States without the presence of African Americans. As Hickman preaches: "They can curse and kill us but they can't destroy us all. This land is ours because we came out of it, we bled in it, our tears watered it, we fertilized it with our dead. So the more of us they destroy the more it becomes filled with the spirit of our redemption." [65] This image of dismembered black bodies watering and fertilizing American soil and then being reborn out of it recurs in Ellison's work. The black body as "seed" is presented in Invisible Man's castration nightmare and in Rev. Hickman's sermon, "Dry Bones in the Valley."

However, even when considering relatively radical or subversive comments made by Invisible Man or Minifees or Rev. Hickman, one must remember that Ellison remained an optimist to the end. That sense of affirmation and possibility about which he writes so frequently and eloquently is also connected to his belief in laughter. Comments he made in his introduction to the thirtieth anniversary edition of *Invisible Man* sum up his position: "Given the persistence of racial violence and the unavailability of legal protection, I asked myself, what else *was* there to sustain our will to persevere but laughter? And could it be that there was a subtle triumph hidden in such laughter that I had missed, but one which still was more affirmative than raw anger? A secret, hard-earned wisdom that might, perhaps, offer a more effective strategy through which a floundering Afro-American novelist could convey his vision?" [66]

Ellison possessed a sense of humor, and it, like his unwavering faith in the promise of democracy, stood him in good stead. To Ellison, jazz was defined by its inherent humor and faith, its studied purpose to make life swing. Whenever he heard Duke Ellington's orchestra perform, Ellison believed that the sound captured and helped create a special American sense of cheer and optimism. Ellison also looked at African American life and found within it a golden vision of human possibility. Where others focused on the terrible aspects of black life — oppression, victimization, discrimination — Ellison reminded us of the marvelous — grace, elegance, laughter, and faith. He heard that sense of transcendent possibility expressed in the bright magic of Louis Armstrong's trumpet sound while Satchmo played, say, "Struttin' with Some Barbecue" or "Between the Devil and the Deep Blue Sea." As a young writer, he dedicated himself to capturing both the marvelous and the terrible. Like Walt Whitman, he believed that the United States was indeed the greatest poem. Ellison gave himself the revisionary assignment of writing the tragicomic predicament of the Negro into the poem. He was faithful to that difficult task from the beginning to the end.

Notes

Jazz States: Ralph Waldo Ellison's Major Chords

1 Ron Wellburn, "Ralph Ellison's Territorial Advantage," in *Conversations with Ralph Ellison*, hereafter cited as *Conversations*, edited by Marryemma Graham and Amritjit Singh (Jackson: University of Mississippi Press, 1995), p. 303.
2 Ellison, "Living with Music," in *The Collected Essays of Ralph Ellison*, hereafter cited as *Collected Essays*, edited by John F. Callahan (New York: Random House, 1995), p. 232.
3 Ellison, "Going to the Territory," *Collected Essays*, p. 605.
4 Welburn, "Ralph Ellison's Territorial Advantage," in *Conversations*, pp. 304–306.
5 Ibid., p. 53.
6 Ibid., p. 54.
7 Nathan Huggins, *Black Odyssey: The African-American Ordeal in Slavery* (New York: Vintage Books, 1990), chap. 3.
8 Berndt Ostendorf, "Ralph Ellison: Anthropology, Modernism, and Jazz," in Robert G. O'Meally, *New Essays on Invisible Man*, hereafter cited as *New Essays* (New York: Cambridge University Press, 1988), pp. 96–97.
9 Ellison, "An Extravagance of Laughter," *Collected Essays*, p. 617.
10 Robert G. O'Meally, *The Craft of Ralph Ellison* (Cambridge: Harvard University Press, 1980), p. 28.
11 *Conversations*, p. 99.
12 O'Meally, *New Essays*, p. 4.
13 *Conversations*, p. 99.
14 Addison Gayle, *The Way of the New World: The Black Novel in America* (Garden City, NY: Anchor Press, 1976), p. 257.
15 Irving Howe, *Selected Writings: 1950–1990* (San Diego: Harcourt Brace Jovanovich, 1990), pp. 119–140.
16 Ellison, "A Very Stern Discipline," *Collected Essays*, pp. 738–739.
17 Ellison, "Going to the Territory," *Collected Essays*, p. 609.
18 Ellison, "Blues People," *Collected Essays*, p. 286.
19 Ellison, "Twentieth-Century Fiction and the Mask of Humanity," *Collected Essays*, p. 85.
20 Ellison, "An Extravagance of Laughter," *Collected Essays*, pp. 622–623.
21 Ellison, "Living with Music," *Collected Essays*, p. 229.
22 Ellison, "The Little Man at Chehaw Station," *Collected Essays*, p. 510.
23 Ibid., p. 511.
24 Ellison, "What America Would Be Like without Blacks," *Collected Essays*, p. 580.
25 Ibid., p. 582.
26 Ellison, "A Completion of Personality," *Collected Essays*, p. 803.
27 Ellison, "The Little Man at Chehaw Station," *Collected Essays*, p. 504.
28 Ellison, "The Novel as A Function of Democracy," *Collected Essays*, p. 763.
29 Ellison, "Perspective of Literature," *Collected Essays*, p. 773.
30 Ellison, "The Little Man at Chehaw Station," *Collected Essays*, p. 501.

31 Ellison, "Going to the Territory," *Collected Essays*, p. 595.
32 Ellison, "The Little Man at Chehaw Station," *Collected Essays*, p. 489.
33 Ibid., pp. 489, 490.
34 Ibid., p. 494.
35 Ibid., p. 493.
36 Ellison, "The World and the Jug," *Collected Essays*, p. 160.
37 Ellison, "A Very Stern Discipline," *Collected Essays*, pp. 737–738.
38 Ellison, "The Art of Fiction," *Collected Essays*, p. 224.
39 Ellison, "Hidden Name and Complex Fate," *Collected Essays*, p. 189.
40 Ellison, "Introduction to the Thirtieth Anniversary Edition of *Invisible Man*," *Collected Essays*, pp. 482–483.

Jazz Essays: Ellison on Charlie Christian, Jimmy Rushing, Mahalia Jackson, and Lester Young

1 Ellison, "Introduction to *Shadow and Act*," *Collected Essays*, pp. 50, 51.
2 Ibid., p. 51.
3 J. A. Rogers, "Jazz at Home," in Alain Locke, *The New Negro* (New York: Atheneum, 1980), p. 27.
4 Alain Locke, *The Negro and His Music* (New York: Arno Press, 1969), p. 97.
5 Ellison, "The Charlie Christian Story," *Collected Essays*, pp. 269–270. See also "What These Children Are Like" (*Collected Essays*, p. 548), a lecture Ellison delivered at a 1963 seminar titled "Education for the Culturally Different Youth," in which he discussed Charlie Christian's life as a case study in American resourcefulness.
6 Ibid., pp. 267–268.
7 Ibid., p. 269.
8 Ibid., p. 271.
9 Ibid., p. 267.
10 Ellison, "Living with Music," *Collected Essays*, p. 229.
11 Ellison, "That Same Pain, That Same Pleasure," *Collected Essays*, p. 67.
12 Ellison, "Remembering Jimmy," *Collected Essays*, pp. 273, 273–274.
13 Ellison, "That Same Pain," p. 67.
14 Ellison, "As the Spirit Moves Mahalia," *Collected Essays*, p. 255.
15 Ibid., pp. 252–253.
16 Max Roach, "What Jazz Means to Me," in *Speech and Power: The Afro-American Essay and Its Cultural Content, from Polemics to Pulpit*, vol. 2, edited by Gerald Early (Hopewell, NJ: Ecco Press, 1993), p. 53.
17 Ellison, "Remembering Jimmy," *Collected Essays*, p. 275.
18 Ellison, "The Charlie Christian Story," *Collected Essays*, p. 272.
19 Mark Gridley, *Jazz Styles: History and Analysis* (Englewood Cliffs, NJ: Prentice Hall, 1991), pp. 101–102.
20 Ellison, "The Charlie Christian Story," *Collected Essays*, p. 272.
21 Mark Gridley, *Jazz Styles*, pp. 132–134.
22 Benny Green, *The Reluctant Art: Five Studies in the Growth of Jazz* (New York: Da Capo Press, 1962), p. 101.
23 Ellison, "The Charlie Christian Story," *Collected Essays*, p. 262.
24 Ibid., p. 266.

25 *Conversations with Ralph Ellison*, pp. 310–311.

26 Ted Gioia, *The History of Jazz* (New York: Oxford University Press, 1998), p. 154.

27 Ibid., p. 138.

28 Ellison, "What America Would Be Like without Blacks," *Collected Essays*, p. 580.

29 Gioia, *History of Jazz*, p. 108.

30 Ibid., pp. 108–109.

31 Green, *Reluctant Art*, pp. 95–96.

32 John Hasse, *Beyond Category: The Life and Genius of Duke Ellington* (New York: Simon and Schuster, 1993), p. 195.

33 *Conversations with Ralph Ellison*, p. 314.

34 Gioia, *History of Jazz*, p. 66.

Jazz Icons: Ellison on Duke Ellington, Louis Armstrong, and Charlie Parker

1 Ellison, "Homage to Duke Ellington," *Collected Essays*, p. 678.

2 Ibid., pp. 678–679.

3 Hasse, *Beyond Category*, p. 400.

4 For a thorough discussion of Ellington's early life, see Hasse, *Beyond Category*, chap. 1. In "Homage to Duke Ellington" (*Collected Essays*, p. 676), Ellison wrote: "President Richard M. Nixon has ordered in his [Ellington's] honor a state dinner to be served in the house where, years ago, Duke's father, then a butler, once instructed white guests from the provinces in the gentle art and manners proper to such places of elegance and power. . . . And perhaps it is inevitable that Duke Ellington should be shown the highest hospitality of the nation's First Family in its greatest house, and that through the courtesy of the chief of state all Americans may pay, symbolically, their respects to our greatest composer."

5 Hasse, *Beyond Category*, p. 23.

6 Gary Giddins, *Visions of Jazz: The First Century* (New York: Oxford University Press, 1998), p. 107.

7 Ellison, "Homage to Duke Ellington," p. 679.

8 Ibid., p. 680.

9 Stanley Crouch, *Always in Pursuit* (New York: Pantheon Books, 1998), p. 49.

10 Gene Fernett, *Swing Out: Great Negro Jazz Bands* (New York: Da Capo Press, 1993), p. 11.

11 Mark Tucker, *The Duke Ellington Reader* (New York: Oxford University Press, 1993), p. 458.

12 Ibid., pp. 466–467.

13 Ellison, "Homage to Duke Ellington," p. 679.

14 Ibid., p. 680.

15 Ibid.

16 Ibid., p. 681.

17 Ibid.

18 Hasse, *Beyond Category*, pp. 176–185.

19 Tucker, *The Duke Ellington Reader*, pp. 451–453.
20 Hasse, *Beyond Category*, pp. 176–178.
21 Shane White and Graham White, *Stylin': African American Expressive Culture from Its Beginning to the Zoot Suit* (Ithaca, NY: Cornell University Press, 1998), p. 244.
22 Laurence Bergreen, *Louis Armstrong: An Extravagant Life* (New York: Broadway Books, 1997), pp. 478–479.
23 Fernett, *Swing Out*, p. 12.
24 Giddins, *Visions of Jazz*, p. 89.
25 Ibid., pp. 89–90.
26 Gioia, *History of Jazz*, p. 56.
27 Bergreen, *Louis Armstrong*, p. 247.
28 Ibid.
29 Ellison, "The Golden Age, Time Past," *Collected Essays*, p. 247.
30 Ellison, "Change the Joke and Slip the Yoke," *Collected Essays*, pp. 106–107.
31 Ellison, "On Bird, Bird-Watching and Jazz," *Collected Essays*, p. 258.
32 Ibid., p. 263.
33 Ibid., pp. 259–260.
34 Ibid., p. 261.
35 Ibid., p. 262.
36 Ibid., p. 261.
37 Ellison, "The Golden Age, Time Past," p. 242.
38 Ibid., p. 245.
39 Gioia, *History of Jazz*, p. 206.
40 Albert Murray and John Callahan, *Trading Twelves: The Selected Letters of Ralph Ellison and Albert Murray* (New York: Modern Library, 2000), pp. 163–165.
41 Ibid., pp 166–167.
42 Ibid., p. 167.

Jazz Trio: Ralph Ellison, Romare Bearden, and Albert Murray

1 *Conversations with Ralph Ellison*, p. 220.
2 Ibid., p. 368.
3 Calvin Tompkins, "Putting Something over Something Else," in *The Jazz Cadence of American Culture*, edited by Robert O'Meally (New York: Columbia University Press, 1998), p. 224.
4 Ibid., p. 226.
5 Huston Paschal, *Riffs and Takes: Music in the Art of Romare Bearden* (exhibition catalogue, January 23–April 3, 1988) (Raleigh: North Carolina Museum of Art), p. 1.
6 Tomkins, "Putting Something," pp. 236–237.
7 Mona Hadler, "Jazz and the New York School," in *Representing Jazz*, edited by Krin Gabbared (Durham, NC: Duke University Press, 1995), pp. 247–248.
8 Paschal, *Riffs and Takes*, pp. 2–3.
9 Tomkins, "Putting Something," p. 225.

10 Ibid., p. 235.

11 Ibid., p. 238.

12 Cited in Sharon F. Patton, *Memory and Metaphor: The Art of Romare Bearden, 1940–1987* (New York: Oxford University Press, 1991), p. 44.

13 Albert Murray, *The Blue Devils of Nada* (New York: Vintage, 1997), p. 126.

14 Myron Schwartzman, *Romare Bearden: His Life and Art* (New York: Harry N. Abrams, 1990), p. 107.

15 Ibid., pp. 195–196, 195.

16 Ibid., p. 202.

17 Ibid., pp. 202–203.

18 Ellison, "The Art of Romare Bearden," *Collected Essays*, p. 684.

19 Ibid., p. 685.

20 Ibid., pp 685–686.

21 Schwartzman, *Romare Bearden*, p. 197.

22 Ellison, "The Art of Romare Bearden," *Collected Essays*, p. 687.

23 Romare Bearden, "The Negro Artist and Modern Art," in Gerald Early, *Speech and Power* (Hopewell, NJ: Ecco Press, 1993), p. 11.

24 Patton, *Memory and Metaphor*, p. 38.

25 Ibid., p. 43.

26 Schwartzman, *Romare Bearden*, p. 27.

27 Ibid., p. 34.

28 Ellison, "The Art of Romare Bearden," *Collected Essays*, p. 690.

29 Ellison, "That Same Pain, That Same Pleasure," *Collected Essays*, pp. 78–79.

30 Ellison, "The Art of Romare Bearden," *Collected Essays*, p. 693.

31 Roberta S. Maguire, ed., *Conversations with Albert Murray* (Jackson: University of Mississippi Press, 1997), pp. 90–91.

32 Murray, *Blue Devils of Nada*, p. 101.

33 Mark Feeney, "The Unsquarest Person Duke Ellington Ever Met," in Maguire, *Conversations with Albert Murray*, p. 70.

34 Ibid.

35 Albert Murray, "The Function of the Heroic Image," in O'Meally, *Jazz Cadence*, p. 571.

36 Ibid., p. 571.

37 Ibid., pp. 571–572.

38 Ellison, "A Very Stern Discipline," *Collected Essays*, p. 738.

39 Murray, "The Function of the Heroic Image," p. 572.

40 Ibid., p. 574.

41 Albert Murray, *Stomping the Blues* (New York: Vintage, 1982), pp. 250–251.

42 Ibid., p. 82.

43 Murray and Callahan, *Trading Twelves*, p. 191.

44 Murray, *Blue Devils*, p. 98.

45 Murray, *Stomping*, p. 148.

46 Murray, *Blue Devils*, p. 108.

47 Ibid., p. 109.

48 Ibid., pp. 109–110, 111.

49 James Baldwin, "The Harlem Ghetto," in *The Price of the Ticket* (New York: St. Martin's Press, 1985), p. 1.

50 Ibid.

51 Albert Murray, *The Omni-Americans: Some Alternatives to Folklore of White Supremacy* (New York: Vintage, 1970), p. 149.

52 Ellison, "Harlem Is Nowhere," *Collected Essays*, p. 320.

53 Ibid., p. 321.

54 Ellison, "Harlem Is Nowhere," pp. 321–322.

55 Ellison, "An Extravagance of Laughter," *Collected Essays*, p. 615.

56 Murray, *Blue Devils*, p. 140.

57 Tomkins, "Putting Something," p. 240.

58 Ellison, "The Art of Romare Bearden," p. 692.

59 Murray and Callahan, *Trading Twelves*, p. 20.

60 Ibid., pp. 20–21.

61 Ibid., p. 21.

Jazz Underground: *Invisible Man* as Jazz Text

1 Ralph Ellison, *Invisible Man* (New York: Modern Library, 1994), pp. 7–8.

2 O'Meally, *New Essays*, p. 11.

3 Ellison, *Conversations*, pp. 93–94.

4 Eric Sundquist, *Cultural Contexts for Ralph Ellison's Invisible Man* (Boston: Bedford Books of St. Martin's Press, 1995), pp. 11–12.

5 Henry Louis Gates, Jr., *The Signifying Monkey: A Theory of African-American Literary Criticism* (New York: Oxford University Press, 1989), p. 131.

6 *Invisible Man*, p. xxii.

7 O'Meally, *New Essays*, p. 2.

8 W. E. B. Du Bois, *The Souls of Black Folk*, in *The Norton Anthology of African American Literature* (New York: W. W. Norton, 1997), p. 615.

9 W. E. B. Du Bois, *Dusk of Dawn: An Essay towards an Autobiography of a Race Concept* (New York: Schocken Books, 1968), pp. 130–131.

10 *Invisible Man*, p. 9.

11 Ellison, "Golden Age, Time Past," *Collected Essays*, p. 245.

12 *Invisible Man*, p. 192.

13 *Invisible Man*, p. 205.

14 Ellison, "Hidden Name and Complex Fate," *Collected Essays*, p. 199.

15 Ellison, "A Completion of Personality," *Collected Essays*, p. 803.

16 *Invisible Man*, p. 212.

17 *Invisible Man*, pp. 265–266.

18 See Ellison, "What America Would Be Like without Blacks," *Collected Essays*, pp. 578–579, for his comments on Garvey's movement.

19 *Invisible Man*, p. 266.

20 Ibid.

21 Ibid., p. 273.

22 Ibid., p. 374.

23 Ibid., p. 434.

24 Ibid., p. 436.

25 Genevieve Fabre and Robert G. O'Meally, eds., *History and Memory in African-American Culture* (New York: Oxford University Press, 1964), p. 20.

26 Nat Brandt, *Harlem at War: The Black Experience in World War II* (Syracuse,

NY: Syracuse University Press, 1996), pp. 183–206. Ellison was named as an eyewitness to the riot in a story that appeared in the *New York Post* on August 2, 1943. The reporter wrote: "One eyewitness of many lootings, Ralph Ellison, managing editor of the *Negro Quarterly*, said that only stores owned by white persons were looted."

27 Ellison, "The Art of Romare Bearden," *Collected Essays*, pp. 692–693.
28 *Invisible Man*, pp. 526–529.
29 Ibid., p. 530.
30 Ibid., p. 535.
31 Ibid., p. 545.
32 Ibid., p. 547.
33 Ibid., pp. 549–550.
34 Ibid., p. 559.
35 Ibid., p. 560.
36 Ibid., p. 561.
37 Ibid., p. 560.
38 Ibid., p. 561.
39 Ibid., p. 93.
40 Ibid., p. 205.
41 Ibid., p. 561.
42 Ibid.
43 Ibid., p. 570.

Jazz in Progress: *Juneteenth*, Ellison's Second Novel

1 *Invisible Man*, p. 6.
2 Ibid., p. 564.
3 Ralph Ellison, *Juneteenth* (New York: Random House, 1999). See John F. Callahan's introduction, pp. xi–xxiii.
4 Louis Menand, "Unfinished Business," *New York Times Book Review*, June 20, 1999, pp. 4–6.
5 Peter Monaghan, "Finishing Ralph Ellison's Second Novel," *Chronicle of Higher Education*, July 14, 1995, p. A5.
6 Ellison, "A Completion of Personality," *Collected Essays*, pp. 790–791.
7 Ellison, "Cadillac Flambé," in *American Review 16*, edited by Theodore Solotaroff (New York: Bantam Books, 1973), pp. 249–269.
8 Ibid., pp. 264–265.
9 O'Meally, "On Burke and the Vernacular: Ralph Ellison's Boomerang of History," in *History and Memory*, p. 249.
10 Ellison, "Cadillac Flambé," p. 268.
11 Ibid., p. 250.
12 Ibid., p. 251.
13 Ellison, *Conversations with Ralph Ellison*, p. 329.
14 Crouch, *Always in Pursuit*, p. 132.
15 Ellison, "Cadillac Flambé," p. 254.
16 Ibid.
17 Ibid., p. 259.
18 Ibid., p. 265.

19 Ibid., p. 262.
20 Ibid., pp. 263–264.
21 Ibid., p. 263.
22 Ibid., p. 268.
23 Ibid., p. 267.
24 Ibid., p. 268.
25 Ibid., p. 265.
26 Ibid., p. 266.

Jazz Preaching: Reverend Hickman and the Battered Silver Trombone

1   James Weldon Johnson, *God's Trombones: Seven Negro Sermons in Verse* (1927) (New York: Viking, 1969), pp. 1–11.
2   Ibid., pp. 4–7.
3   Ellison, *Conversations*, p. 220.
4   Richard Lischer, *The Preacher King: Martin Luther King and the Word That Moved America* (New York: Oxford University Press, 1995), pp. 120–121.
5   Ellison, *Conversations*, p. 329.
6   Jeff Todd Titon, *Give Me This Mountain: Rev. C. L. Franklin: Life, History, and Selected Sermons* (Urbana: University of Illinois Press, 1989), p. 4.
7   Ben Sidran, *Talking Jazz: An Illustrated Oral History* (San Francisco: Pomegranate, 1992), p. 144.
8   *Juneteenth*, pp. 116–117.
9   Gridley, *Jazz Styles*, p. 118.
10 *Juneteenth*, p. 117.
11 Ibid.
12 Ibid., p. 118.
13 Ibid.
14 Ibid.
15 Ibid., p. 119.
16 Countee Cullen, "Heritage," in *Norton Anthology of African American Literature*, p. 1312.
17 *Juneteenth*, p. 121.
18 Ibid., p. 122.
19 Ibid.
20 Titon, *Give Me This Mountain*, p. 43.
21 *Juneteenth*, p. 124.
22 Ibid., p. 125.
23 Ellison, "As the Spirit Moves Mahalia," *Collected Essays*, p. 255.
24 T. S. Eliot, *The Complete Poems of T. S. Eliot, 1909–1950* (New York: Harcourt, Brace, and World, 1971), p. 38.
25 *Juneteenth*, pp. 126–127.
26 Titon, *Give Me This Mountain*, pp. 85–86.
27 Benston, *Speaking for You*, p. 305.
28 *Juneteenth*, p. 127.
29 Ibid.
30 Ibid., p. 128.

31 Ellison, "Blues People," *Collected Essays*, pp. 283–284.
32 Ellison, "Perspective of Literature," *Collected Essays*, p. 773.
33 Titon, *Give Me This Mountain*, pp. 87–88.
34 Ibid., p. 88.
35 *Juneteenth*, p. 129.
36 Duke Ellington, "It Don't Mean a Thing If It Ain't Got That Swing," *Norton Anthology of African-American Literature*, p. 38.
37 Ellison, *Juneteenth*, p. 131.
38 Ibid., p. 124.

Jazz Trumpet No End: Ellison's Riffs with Irving Howe and Other Critics

1 Ellison, "A Very Stern Discipline," *Collected Essays*, p. 740.
2 Norman Mailer, *Advertisements for Myself* (New York: Putnam, 1959), pp. 433–434.
3 Norman Podhoretz, "The Melting Pot Blues," *Washington Post Book Week*, October 25, 1964, p. 3.
4 Ibid.
5 Norman Podhoretz, *Breaking Ranks* (New York: Harper and Row, 1979), p. 133.
6 Jerry Watts, *Heroism and the Black Intellectual: Ralph Ellison, Politics, and Afro-American Intellectual Life* (Chapel Hill: University Press of North Carolina, 1994), pp. 93–95.
7 Ellison, "A Very Stern Discipline," *Collected Essays*, p. 741.
8 Ellison, "The Myth," *Collected Essays*, p. 553.
9 Ellison, "The World and the Jug," *Collected Essays*, pp. 164–65.
10 See Maguire, *Conversations with Ralph Ellison*, p. 99.
11 Baldwin's essay originally appeared in the *New Yorker* before being published as a book and becoming a bestseller.
12 James Baldwin, "The Fire Next Time," in *The Price of the Ticket*, p. 379.
13 Irving Howe, "Black Boys and Native Sons," *Selected Writings*, p. 121.
14 Ibid., pp. 121–122.
15 Ellison, "The World and the Jug," *Collected Essays*, p. 185.
16 Watts, "The Responsibilities of the Black Writer," *Heroism*, chap. 3.
17 Ibid., pp. 66. In *Irving Howe: Socialist, Critic, Jew* (Bloomington: Indiana University Press, 1998), pp. 119–131, Edward Alexander paints a complex portrait of Howe, born Irving Horenstein, and his public debates on literature, politics, and Jewish identity with such Jewish writers as Lionel Trilling and Philip Roth.
18 Howe, "Black Boys and Native Sons," *Selected Writings*, p. 131.
19 Ellison, "The Art of Fiction," *Collected Essays*, pp. 211–212.
20 Howe, "Black Boys and Native Sons," *Selected Writings*, pp. 125–126.
21 Ellison, "The Art of Romare Bearden," *Collected Essays*, p. 692.
22 Ellison, "Harlem Is Nowhere," *Collected Essays*, p. 322.
23 Ellison, "The World and the Jug," pp. 159–160.
24 Howe, "Black Boys and Native Sons," *Selected Writings*, pp. 131–132.
25 *Invisible Man*, p. 4.

26 James Baldwin, "Everybody's Protest Novel," in *The Price of the Ticket*, pp. 28–30.
27 Langston Hughes, "The Negro Artist and the Racial Mountain," in Gerald Early, *Speech and Power*, vol. 1, p. 91.
28 Ellison, "The World and the Jug," *Collected Essays*, p. 169.
29 Howe, "Black Boys and Native Sons," *Selected Writings*, pp. 119–139.
30 Ellison, "The World and the Jug," *Collected Essays*, p. 163.
31 Ibid., p. 164.
32 Richard Wright, *Black Boy* (New York: Harper and Row, 1966), pp. 271–273.
33 Ellison, "Richard Wright's Blues," *Collected Essays*, p. 129.
34 Ellison, "A Very Stern Discipline," *Collected Essays*, p. 733.
35 Ellison, "Remembering Richard Wright," *Collected Essays*, p. 667.
36 Ibid., pp. 670–671.
37 Ellison, "The Art of Fiction," *Collected Essays*, p. 211.
38 Ellison, "Hidden Name and Complex Fate," *Collected Essays*, p. 205, 206.
39 Ellison, "Brave Words for a Startling Occasion," *Collected Essays*, p. 153.
40 Ellison, "Introduction to the Thirtieth Anniversary Edition of *Invisible Man*," *Collected Essays*, p. 482.
41 Watts, *Heroism*, p. 75.
42 Ibid., p. 83.
43 Ibid., p. 104.
44 Ibid., p. 106.
45 Ibid., pp. 106–107.
46 Ellison, "The Charlie Christian Story," *Collected Essays*, p. 270.
47 Watts, *Heroism*, p. 155.
48 Ellison, "Blues People," *Collected Essays*, p. 284.
49 Ellison, "A Completion of Personality," *Collected Essays*, p. 803.
50 Ellison, "A Very Stern Discipline," *Collected Essays*, p. 737.
51 Ibid., p. 747.
52 Watts, *Heroism*, pp. 114, 120.
53 Norman Podhoretz, "Whatever Happened to Ralph Ellison," *Commentary*, July-August 1999, p. 56.
54 Ibid.
55 Murray, *Trading Twelves*, p. 117.
56 Ellison, "A Very Stern Discipline," *Collected Essays*, pp. 732–733.
57 Ellison, *Conversations*, p. 136.
58 Larry Neale, "Ellison's Zoot Suit," in *Ralph Ellison*, edited by John Hersey (Englewood Cliffs, NJ: Prentice Hall, 1974), pp. 71–72.
59 Ellison, "A Completion of Personality," *Collected Essays*, p. 801.
60 Murray, *Trading Twelves*, p. 19.
61 James Baldwin, "Why I Stopped Hating Shakespeare" (uncollected essay).
62 Ellison, "Perspective of Literature," *Collected Essays*, pp. 777–778.
63 *Invisible Man*, p. 550.
64 Ellison, "Cadillac Flambé," p. 268.
65 Ellison, *Juneteenth*, p. 130.
66 Ellison, "Introduction," *Collected Essays*, p. 478.

Index

minstrel tradition, 22
Minton's (jazz club), 47
Moby-Dick (Melville), 15
modernist themes, 76–77
Mondrian, Piet, 52
Monk, Thelonious, 47
Montgomery, Wes, 26
"Mood Indigo" (Ellington), 65
Moore, Marianne, 62
Morton, Benny, 29
Moten, Benny, 3
Moynihan, Daniel Patrick, 10
"Mr. Five by Five" (Rushing). See Rushing, Jimmy
Murray, Albert: correspondence with Ellison, 47, 141–42, 143–44; on distinctiveness, 87; Ellison's friendship with, 1; as renaissance man, 49–51; writings of, 61–71
music, ritualistic, 116. See also blues; jazz
Music Is My Mistress (Murray), 65–66
My Bondage and My Freedom (Douglass), 81

Nanton, Joseph "Tricky Sam," 36, 37, 55, 110
National Book Award, 5, 123, 132
National Newspaper Publishers' Award, 5
nationalism (Black nationalism), 138
Native Son (Wright), 124, 125, 127, 135
Neale, Larry, 142–43
The Negro and His Music (Locke), 19
"The Negro Artist and Modern Art" (Bearden), 58
"The Negro Artist and the Racial Mountain" (Hughes), 128
"negro" compared to "black," 137
Negro Digest, 57
Negro folklore, 15
Nehru, Jawaharlal, 130
New Essays on Invisible Man (O'Meally), 5, 76
New Leader, 122

The New Negro (Locke), 19
New York City, 4–5, 37, 76. See also Harlem
New York Post, 154–55n. 26
New York Review of Books, 138
New York Times Book Review, 92–93
Nixon, Richard, 151n. 4
"A Note to Scholars" (Callahan), 93
Notes from the Underground (Dostoevsky), 125
Notes of a Native Son (Baldwin), 129
"The Novel as a Function of Democracy" (Ellison), 12, 131

Oedipus Rex (Sophocles), 125
Oklahoma City, Oklahoma: Armstrong in, 30–31, 40–41, 51; Ellington in, 33, 37, 51; Ellison's youth in, 17–18, 21; Harlem compared to, 67; jazz culture of, 3; "wild" state of, 20
Oliver, King, 3, 43
O'Meally, Robert, 5, 76, 96
The Omni-Americans: New Perspectives on Black Experience and American Culture (Murray), 62, 67
"On Bird, Bird-Watching, and Jazz" (Ellison), 44
optimism of Ellison, 146
orchestras, cultural significance of, 35
Orozco, José, 59
Ory, Kid, 43
Ostendorf, Berndt, 4

Page, Oran "Hot Lips," 3
Page, Walter, 3
Paris Blues (motion picture), 65
Paris, France, 69
Parker, Charlie, 1, 2, 42–48
"Perspective of Literature" (Ellison), 117
The Piano Lesson (Bearden), 59
Picasso, Pablo, 55, 87
"playing the dozens," 100
pluralism, 10, 13, 121
Podhoretz, Norman, 2, 121, 140–41
poetic closure, 92–94
Poitier, Sidney, 65

political incorrectness of Ellison, 137–47

Pollock, Jackson, 52

popular culture, 10–11, 80, 134–35, 142, 143. See also culture

populist values, 7

Porter, Cole, 53

A Portrait of the Artist (Joyce), 130

possibility as a theme in Ellison's work, 8, 9–10, 89

The Preacher King: Martin Luther King and the Word That Moved America (Lischer), 107

preachers and preaching, 105–109, 114–17, 118, 146. See also "The Valley of the Dry Bones"

prejudice, 18, 40–41, 53, 98

Primus Provo, 81–82

protest, 59, 125

Pulitzer Prize Committee, 33, 38, 39

"Putting Something over Something Else" (Tompkins), 50

race riots, 72–76, 127

racism, 102

radical, Ellison as, 7–8

Rainey, Ma, 1, 3

"Ralph Waldo Ellison: Anthropology, Modernism and Jazz" (Ostendorf), 4

Randolph, Jefferson Davis, 78

Ras the Exhorter, 85–86, 127, 145

rebirth, 116

"Rectangular Structure in My Montage Paintings" (Bearden), 59

redemption as a theme in Ellison's work, 89–90, 146

Redman, Don, 43, 52

Reinhardt, Django, 26

religion. See preachers and preaching

"Remembering Jimmy" (Ellison), 23

"Remembering Richard Wright" (Ellison), 130

renaissance men, 17–18

responsibility of African American artists, 139

Rhapsody in Black and Blue (motion picture), 45

"Richard Wright's Blues" (Ellison), 19, 64, 130

riots: absurdity and, 85–87; Ellison as witness to, 154–55n. 26; Harlem Riot, 72–76, 83–91, 127, 145; Tulsa riot, 23

Rivera, Diego, 59

Rivers, Larry, 52

Roach, Max, 25, 55

Rocket to the Moon (Bearden), 61

Rogers, J. A., 19

Rourke, Constance, 32

Rushing, Jimmy, 1, 2, 22–25, 83–84, 114

Satchmo. See Armstrong, Louis

Saturday Review, 18, 19

Savoy Ballroom, 52

"Seabreeze" (song), 53

segregation: artistic freedom and, 128–29; Du Bois on, 77; Howe on, 123; ironies of, 12; jazz music and, 40–42, 136–37; Stern on, 60

self-destruction of Parker, 46

self-knowledge, 109–10

Seurat, 55

Shadow and Act (Ellison): Ellison's childhood in, 129; introduction to, 3–4, 17; Podhoretz on, 140–41; review of, 121; significance of, 2

Shakespeare, William, 144

Sheiks of Araby, 41–42

Sidran, Ben, 17

signifying, 75

The Signifying Monkey: A Theory of African-American Literary Criticism (Gates), 75

Slaughter's Hall, 24

slavery: dancing, 38–39; Ellington on, 105; personified in Invisible Man, 80–81; sermons on, 111–13; transcendence and, 138–39

"Slick Gonna Learn" (Ellison), 5

Smith, Bessie, 47, 52

Smith, Buster, 3

Smith, Clara, 3, 52